COLLECTION DEVELOPMENT

Its Organization and Services in University Libraries

COLLECTION DEVELOPMENT

Its Organization and Services in University Libraries

By
Abdul Mannan Khan

Ess Ess Publications
New Delhi

Collection Development

Its Organization and Services in University Libraries

ISBN: 978-81-7000-684-8

Rs.700/-

First Published 2013

Published by:
Ess Ess Publications
4831/24, Ansari Road,
Darya Ganj,
New Delhi-110 002.
INDIA
Phones: 23260807, 41563444
Fax: 41563334
E-mail: info@essessreference.com
www.essessreference.com

Cover Design by *Patch Creative Unit*

Printed and bound in India at Salasar Imaging Systems.

Dedicated to

my

PARENTS & GRAND PARENTS

whose blessings and benedictions are

Academic sinews for me

Contents

Foreword

The practice of selection of reading materials for libraries is as old as the existence of libraries done themselves. But records of how it was in the ancient libraries of Alexandria, Pergamum, Nalanda and Taxila are not available. The rarity of material and their value as unique records of comprehensive knowledge of human being, and its preservation for future generations were perhaps the guiding principles in making their selection; Libraries were served primarily as storehouses than institutions for dissemination of knowledge. Making collection for completeness and preservation remain continued as the principal goals of libraries. The invention of printing press, followed by increasing literacy resulting in the demand for books, expansion of public library movement and subsequently the proliferation of electronic resources have greatly influenced the role of libraries from time to time.

Till the beginning the twentieth century systematic philosophies of book selection was very rare. Completeness was the goal and it was balanced by the desire to select the best to the largest number at the least cost. However, appropriate criteria for selection has been a topic for continuing debate among librarians and their users for centuries.

The term collection development came into use in the early 1970s to replace selection as a wider range of meaning reflecting the process of developing a library collection in response to the needs of the users, priorities of the institution and its interests. Collection development, now, must be understood to cover several activities related to the development of library collection, viz., selection, assessment of the users' needs, use and user studies, collection analysis, budget management, community outreach and liaison, planning for resource sharing, decisions about weeding and withdrawals, cancelling serials, problems related to storage and preservation. It is also concerned with the determination of selection policy and the assignment of responsibilities for its implementation within the organization.

Collection means the holdings of materials. The Collection Building now stands for the development of several types of documents and special materials in addition to books as principal constituents. 'Collection Development' and 'Collection Building' are the two terms, usually used synonymously, but 'Collection Management' differs slightly. Collection Building now stands for selection and acquisition of materials for libraries considering users current needs and future requirements, where as Collection Management involves managing the use of library collection, its storage, its organization, and this making the collection accessible to users.

I see this book of Dr. Abdul Mannan Khan will serve as an introduction to the topic for both students and practicing librarians with new insight in to the intricacies associated with the Collection Development and help those associated with the responsibilities of performing collection development and management.

Dusshera, 2012 **Prof N. R. Satyanarayana**

Preface

The basic purpose of a library is to preserve knowledge available in any documentary form. University libraries acquire documents to provide information of different hues to satisfy the changing needs of the users i.e. the students, faculty members and the researchers. As a mater of fact, the major objective of libraries has now been transformed from preservation to providing information to the utmost satisfaction of the users. In fact, the entire mechanism of garnering the requisite materials and their proper organization and provision of services is known as collection development, organization and service management.

The richness of collection development, germane organizational pattern and provision of comprehensive ,varied and rich services in fact speak volumes as regards development of Academic Libraries in general and University Libraries in particular. The unfolding of globalization in tandem with the dissemination of knowledge and information has elevated the role of university libraries to a higher level. It has now been undoubtedly acknowledged that the dissemination of quality knowledge of its human capital.

More recently, the concept of Knowledge Process Outsourcing (KPS) has gained wider currency at global level. India is now regarded as a great knowledge provider in the domain of IT and its Enabled Services only on the account of availability of quality knowledge personnel. In order to produce quality human capital including teachers, lawyers, accountants, scientists, managers, executives, researchers and the students, the role of libraries is becoming more and more significant. For dissemination of quality knowledge, quality information is a sine-qua-non. For quality information, the availability of information resources in terms of books, journals, periodicals, reports, non-book materials is indispensable. Obtaining these materials and organizing them systematically and making them available to the users' including the knowledge workers now constitute the core arenas of all academic libraries.

The Information Technology (IT) can extensively be used in libraries and information centres to achieve excellence in the field of research and education. The library has metamorphically converted the traditional repositories of knowledge into powerhouse of knowledge that are able to create, distribute and access information resources through computer networks.

The present study specifically deals with the policy aspects and dimensions of collection development, organization and services from the view points of the librarians as well as the users including faculty members, research scholars and the post graduate students. The study has been made meaningful by taking up the studies of select central university libraries.

Abdul Mannan Khan

Acknowledgements

I sincerely offer my prayer to the ALMIGHTY ALLAH for bestowing on me the greatest mercifulness and the choicest blessings without which I could have never completed this book. During the preparation of this volume I have received the endless and constant support from my parents Mr. Mohd. Farooque Khan Shahiul-Quadri and Mrs. Alfun Nisa and continuous help from my siblings. I am extremely grateful to them. I am also thankful to my wife Gulrez Rana for her unstinted support. I would like to express my utmost gratitude to Syed Mustafa K.Q. Zaidi, Formerly-Chairman, Department of Library and Information Science, Aligarh Muslim University, Aligarh, India for his scholarly guidance; and my special thank to my uncle Prof. Abdul Quayyum Khan' Faculty of Commerce; AMU, Aligarh for his motivation for me for my research and his expert suggestions in application of statistical tools and techniques. I would also like to express my special gratitude to Prof. N.R.Satyanarayana, Former-Dean School of Information Science and Technology, Babasaheb Bhimrao Ambedkar University, Lucknow, for his cooperation and encouragement by writing foreword for this book. Despite of all my best efforts to make the book free from errors, there may be errors still unnoticed for which I take all the responsibility personally.

Abdul Mannan Khan

1

History and Development of University Libraries in India

India has a glorious past being the birthplace of one of the earliest civilizations in the world. There is in fact in no other country where love of learning has so early and its origin and exercising a lasting an influence.[1] Academic institutions were highly significant in India even in ancient period. In the following paragraphs a comprehensive detail is presented as regards the historical almanac of University libraries in India.

UNIVERSITY LIBRARIES IN ANCIENT INDIA

Taxila and Nalanda were known for their well-equipped libraries with a wide and varied manuscript collection.[2] According to a Tibetan account—Nalanda had a grand library called Dharamaganja (Piety Mart). It consisted of three grand buildings called Ratnasagara, Ratnadadhi and Ratnaranjika respectively.[3] Among them, "Ratnasagara" which was a nine-storied building, specialized in the collection of rare and sacred manuscripts on classical literature.[4] The library of this ancient institution of learning was believed to be the biggest in the world. However, despite the growth and expansion, the prestigious Nalanda library could not survive the surge of invaders from the west, particularly the Muslim iconoclasts. It was at the merciless hands of these intruders that Nalanda passed into oblivion and now has become almost a sacred name for the scholars the world over.[5]

Though Taxila was a famous site of learning from 700 B.C. to 300 A.D., no trace of libraries have been found in the archaeological excavations yet. It is believed the reason being that instructions were imparted orally, without using the medium of books.[6] With the advent of Buddhism, teaching came to be practiced through written word and this gave rise to libraries. Fahien noticed such libraries at Jetavana monastery at Sravasti .[7] Jagaddal, Kanhery, Mithila, Odantapuri, Somapuri, Ujjain, Vallabh, and Vikramsila were the other seats of learning which had good collections of manuscripts in the respective libraries attached to them.[8] However, all these libraries were destroyed either by natural calamities or at the hands of the subsequent.[9]

UNIVERSITY LIBRARIES IN MEDIEVAL INDIA

The existence of academic libraries during the medieval period of Indian history is not known. However the medieval period was marked by Sultanates love for books, libraries and knowledge. It is said that the great Persian scholar, Amir Khusro was the librarian of the royal library set up by Jalal-ud-din Khilji.[10] It can, there-fore, be safely concluded that the Sultans regularly maintained libraries in their palaces under the direct aegis of a librarian.[11]

After taking over Delhi's region in 1526, Mughals also patronized penmanship. The first Mughal Emperor, Babar, was a great lover of books; and when he invaded India, he took possession of the personal library of Ghazi Khan. In his own words he "went into Ghazi Khan's room, there were many books of learned contents." Also, he took keen interest in the development of an imperial library as well as his personal library. His son, Humayun, continued the jurisdiction and converted a pleasure-house in Purana Qila of Delhi into a library. Incidentally, a fall from the stairs of his library was the cause of his death.[12]

Akbar, the Great "took much delight in the collection of books in his library. He made several provisions for the good management of his library, and its books were classed under sciences and histories,"[13] Aurangzeb also had mad love for books and knowledge and transferred his library to merge with his palace in Delhi.[14]

UNIVERSITY LIBRARIES IN EARLY NINETEENTH CENTURY

A modern university library has its roots in college libraries. Warren Hastings, Governor-General (1774-85), founded a Madarsa at Calcutta in 1781. Jonathan Duncan in 1792 stressed the need to collect books of the ancient period in order to preserve them for valuable general learning and tradition. Lord Minto, Governor- General (1807-13), in his minutes of the 6 March 1811 wrote "Library be attached to each of the Colleges under the charge of a learned native with a small establishment of servants for the care of manuscripts", .This is probably the first ever statement on record concerning libraries in academic set -up in India. Lord Auckland, Governor-General of India (1836-40), further outlined the library policy in his minutes of the 24 Nov., 1839: In order to make the greatest use of the advantages of the colleges, he said that he would attentively watch the degree to which the students profit by their access to the considerable libraries which are now attached to many of our institutions Important deficiencies in these libraries should be promptly supplied."[15]

After an analysis and evaluation of the college libraries in India, the Hunter Commission (1882) observed that "as regards the extent to which libraries are used, the information obtained seems to show that among the students of some colleges a perceptible taste for general reading has sprung up. Yet, Bombay, Bengal and the North-Western Provinces reports agree in saying that the general reading of students is confined to a very narrow range, being almost entirely limited to the books which have some bearing on the subjects of examinations, though an exception to a limited extent is made in Bombay in the case of the Elphinstone College". Seven years after the Hunter Commission Report in 1889, the Library of the Forman Christian College at Lahore was established.Within five years this Library had a collection of 13,000 books, with a Librarian (H.M, Grawold) to administer it. This library played a prominent role in promoting education among the students. The reading room was opened twenty four hours in a day and promoted self-study. It encouraged inculcation of knowledge beyond the prescribed text-books.[16]

UNIVERSITY LIBRARIES IN MODERN INDIA

During the British rule in India, numbers of academic institutions were established by the East India Company, and by the Christan missionaries. Some of the worth mentioning events which led to the growth and development of higher education in India during this period were the establishment of the Calcutta College in 1781, Jonathan Duncan, then a British agent, founded the Banaras Sanskrit College in 1792.The Calcutta Fort William College was founded in1800. All these colleges were having their own libraries. The Charter Act of 1813, the foundation of Fort William and Serampore Colleges, Calcutta, Madras and Bombay universities and their libraries, Hunter, Raleigh and Calcutta University Commissions, library training programmes, the establishment of Inter University Board, Sargent Report and appointment of the University Grants Committee, the establishment of Madras University, University of Bombay, University of Calcutta and their libraries, the constitution of Inter University Board, the appointment of Hartog Committee, the Montague-Chelmsford reforms of1919, the

Government of India Act of 1935, and the Sargent Committee Report etc. laid foundation for establishment of libraries in various parts of the country.

The Fort William College was founded in Calcutta on18th August 1800 by the Marquis of Welleselay, the Governor-General of India during 1798-1805. Reverend David Brown, Provost of the college was instrumental in setting up the library which had a well rounded collection of Eastern manuscripts. In the absence of adequate financial support, the library could not survive for long and in 1835 it was decided to close the library and its valuable collection was transferred to the Asiatic Society Library in Calcutta between 1835-39.(Kopf, 1969). The Charter Act of 1813 passed by the British Parliament gave the East India Company complete responsibility for educating Indians. The establishment of C.M.S. College in Kottayam, Hindu (Presidency) college in Calcutta in 1816 and Raven Shaw College in Cuttack in 1816 was the immediate result of the Charter Act 1813. These and other colleges came into existence thereafter had their own libraries the day they were established. (Ohdedar, 1969).

Serampore College during this period was founded by the Danes in 1818 and the King of Denmark in 1927agreed to give this college an academic status by providing equivalence to the Danish Universities with power to confer degrees. (Khursheed, 1969). The library of this college too was established along with its foundation and at a later stage the college was given affiliation to the University of Burdwan for the purposeof conferring degrees. (Mathai, 1970)

The 7th March 1835 decision of the British Indian Government to promote English literature and sciences in India was resulted into the spread of number of colleges in India and by 1839 there were over forty colleges with attached libraries in the British territory in India. For their establishment, lots of money was made available by the Indians in the form of donations.(Naik, 1800-1973) In 1840 Presidency College was founded in Madras, followed by a medical college in Bombay in 1845. This progress in education was instrumental in establishing universities in India.

The Charles Wood dispatch of 1854 popularly known as the 'Magna Carta of English Education' in India also paved the way for the establishment of the universities in the presidency towns.(Subramaniam,2001).

Sir John Colville introduced the Bill to establish universities in India and it was passed by the Governor General of India Lord Dalhousie on 24th January 1857, paved the way for the foundation of three universities based on the London Universities Model in the Presidency towns of Calcutta, Madras and Bombay.

Indian Education Commission, popularly known as Hunter Commission was appointed by the British Indian Government in 1882 to study the progress of education under the new policy adopted in 1854 by the East India Company and transferred to the Crown and accepted by the Secretary of State in 1859. (Majumdar, 1946) Sir William W. Hunter in his report had clearly stated that the conditions of the libraries was in a very poor state and declared them "hardly creditable."(Ali, 1967) The Commission paid special attention to the colleges and their libraries and other facilities.

Though the East India Company's Court of Directors earlier rejected the proposal to start universities at Madras and Calcutta in 1834 and 1845 respectively, they yet revised this view due to: (1) the rapid spread of liberal education among Indians; and (2) the requirements of an increased European and Anglo-Indian population. Accordingly, a Despatch (No 49 of 19 July, 1854) was addressed to the Governor- General in Council by Sir Charles Wood. An immediate outcome of this Despatch was the establishment of three affiliating universities at Calcutta, Bombay and Madras in the year 1857 on the model of the London University which itself was an examining body then. According to their preamble these three universities were established for the purpose of ascertaining, by means of examinations, the persons who had acquired proficiency in different branches of literature, science and arts, and of rewarding them by academic degrees as evidence of their respective attainments and marks of honour.[17] Since these universities had no role to play in respect of teaching and research, the need for attaching a library to them immediately after their establishment was not felt.

However, the credit for the establishment of Bombay University Library in the year 1874 which was completed in 1878 and occupied on 27 February, 1880, is attributed to Premchand Roy Chand, who donated Rs. two lakh rupees towards it. At that time it had a small collection of books on history and biography presented to the Library by the Government in 1874. Similarly, Calcutta University Library owes its origin to the philanthropy of Joy Kissan Mookerjee who offered to donate five thousand rupees for purchasing books in the year 1869, but it was not before 1873 that a library was started there. The same was the case with the Madras University Library. In his will, William Griffith transmitted to the University a gift of twenty six thousand five hundred nineteen rupees which was utilized for the establishment of its library in the year 1907.[18]

A major obstacle in the development of these libraries was that they did not serve the primary purpose of the advancement of learning and research. They restricted their activity merely to holding examina-tions and awarding degrees. The teaching work was done by colleges which did not form an integral part of the universities. The universities served as an administration and examination centre where the existence of library was not needed.

UNIVERSITY LIBRARIES IN TWENTIETH CENTURY

With The establishment of Punjab University in the year 1882and Allahabad University in the year 1887, the total number of Universities in India rise to five. However, libraries in these universities were conspicuous by their absence in the priority list of university development. The Report of the Indian Universities Commission of 1902 (Chairman: Sir

Thomas Raleigh) was very critical about this situation, viz,"Of the present university libraries there is not much to be said. The library at Madras appears to be entirely neglected. Bombay has a good collection of oriental and other books; but the library is little used by graduates and hardly at all by students. Calcutta has a library and money has been granted for the purpose of making it supplementary to other libraries in Calcutta. It is opened to fellows and to persons permitted by the Syndicate to use it for the purpose of literary search. The Allahabad University has no library. Lahore has not a very large University Library".[19]

Furthermore, the Commission recommended that good reference libraries should be provided in connection both with universities and colleges in order that students may have an opportunity of forming the habit of independent and intelligent reading.[20]

In the year 1917 Calcutta University Commission highlighted the libraries and their pitiable and pathetic states. The Com-mission remarked that some libraries here and there may be exceptions but "in general the libraries are quite inadequate for the needs of the students, and still more for those of teachers.[21] It has, in its findings, recommended that training should be given to students and teachers towards use of the libraries to strengthen the library system. It further recommended that adequate facilities for teaching function would facilitate great libraries.[22]

UNIVERSITY LIBRARIES DURING 1919-1947

Eight new universities along with their associated libraries were established during the period 1919-1930. There were international contacts between Indian and British university libraries, and gradually with American university libraries as well. The administrative set-up of Indian university libraries was on the basis of the model of the western libraries.[23] After 1921, upgradation of colleges to universities took place that had some kind of libraries attached to them, for instance; the Aligarh Muslim University

(1921) was one of the few colleges which had taken the initiative in establishing a library.[24]

The years between 1939 and 1947, shadowed by World War II, were bleak so far as university library development was concerned. Only two universities, Utkal in 1943 and Saagar in 1946 could be established during this eight-year period.[25] The 20th century provided Indians the opportunity for interaction with librarians in the western countries. This paved way for innovations and improvements, such as open access. The foremost notable example is that of Dr. S.R. Ranganathan provision of card catalogues, subject bibliographies, reference service and inter-library loans as essential features of library service.[26] Also, many India university librarians went to England and America in particu-lar, to study librarianship. They brought back rich library experiences based on their close observations of western libraries and study of new methods and techniques of library services. The knowledge and experience, they earned benefited the functioning of their respective and other university libraries in the country in general.

Many western librarians of prominence posted in India, particularly during the Second World War, also helped in "widening the horizons of library service".[27] But then this was only like a drop in the ocean. Though the changes were characteristi-cally slow the development of libraries continued up to 1947, when India got Independence.

However, the job of a librarian was not considered a respectable one and therefore, did not attract many people. Besides, the librarians were regarded as custodians and were even penalised for loss of books. As a result, the librarians did not perform their duties truly and they neither encouraged the use of books nor took interest in their job. Practically, they did not offer any library services, such as, refe-rence service, bibliographical service, etc. The documentation service was, however, unknown to most of them. Thus, the services of these libraries were deplorable.[28] The entire system of recruitment of librarians was in disarray where under - qualified individuals were appointed to the jobs that were devoid of professionally training.[29] As a result, in some university libraries, an honorary librarian, usually one of the professors, was appointed over the library staff as 'Professor-Incharge of library.[30] This deprived the librarians of all initia-tives, and rather infused in them an attitude of inferiority com-plex. Moreover, it did not attract others to take up a librarian's job. Inevitably it had its adverse effects on the overall library image, as the "professor-in-charge" could not understand the professional duties and restrained the library staff from innovations and development.[31]

It can safely be concluded that the concept of library was a mere formality in the pre-independence period. As a result of which, libraries even in the most well-established universities were not properly organized and the status of the librarians was pitifully low.[32]

UNIVERSITY LIBRARIES IN POST-INDEPENDENCE ERA

After Independence vigorous efforts were made to improve the quality and standard of higher education; particularly at university level. The Government of India in this direction appointed the University Education Commission in 1948, with the eminent philosopher and educationist, Dr. S. Radhakrishnan as its Chairman. The Commission enquired into the existing conditions of university education and made important recommendations to bring it to the level of universities abroad. The importance it accorded to university libraries can be well verified by the following statement of the Commission[33], viz., "The Library is the heart of all the University's work; so as regards its research work, and indirectly as regards its educational work, which derives its life from research work. Scientific research needs a library as well as its laboratories, while for humanistic research the library is both library and laboratory in one."This Commission, however, did not suggest measures to give to the library and the librarian the place they deserved. And to embark upon a programme of university education without assigning due place to the library in the educational set-up sounded like "staging Hamlet without the Prince of

Denmark"[34] In other words, it listed the problem but did not make any suggestions for improvement.

The University Education Commission recommendations paved the way for establishment of the University Grants Commission (UGC) which was set up in the year 1953 and was made a statutory body in the year 1956.[35] The UGC, under its first Chairman, Dr. C.D. Deshmukh, infused new life into the otherwise stagnant college and university libraries.

The University Grants Commission (UGC) appointed a Library Committee, headed by Dr. S.R. Ranganathan,[36] in the year 1957 to advise it on matters relating to the proper functioning and management of college and university libraries. The Committee submitted its Report[37] in 1959, making suitable recommendations on: areas like "grants to libraries; book purchase; reading habits; documentation work; departmental libraries; library personnel; library buildings and furniture."[38]The UGC accepted most of the recommendations of this Committee and provided liberal grants to universities for uplifting their libraries from their pitiable conditions. However, the implementation of the recommendations was selective as the universities were under the state control and accepting them was not compulsory or binding.

The Education Commission, (1964-66) under the Chairmanship of D.S. Kothari observed that "With ever-increasing enrolment in the universities and colleges, the demand for library service has been mounting. Unlike in the past, the library staffs have now to cater to the diverse needs of under-graduates, post-graduates and research scholars. The need for documentation work and service was felt by the Commission due to the tremendous increase in sources of information and also due to the growth in research potential in universities. The Commission, therefore, recommended the appointment of teams of documentalists in university libraries who could understand the requirements of research workers and undertake the work of documentation—search, indexing and abstracting".[39] The Commission also emphasized on student-oriented education: reiterating that "as one goes up, the contact hours could be less and self-study periods longer. The most urgent reform needed, therefore, is to increase the self-study facilities for students. To make it possible well-kept and commodious libraries with adequate number of reading seats is necessary".[40]

All the Commissions on university education have, in fact, "treated the library as subordinate to research, but not a process that should penetrate the academic life of a university campus; and it has never been considered to bring the library into full participation in the teaching process."[41] Financial and professional support from foreign agencies, such as, the British Council Commonwealth Foundation played an important part in the development of Indian libraries and library professionals.[42]

One of the most remarkable and identifiable development in the history of higher education and libraries was the foundation of the INFLIBNET in1991. Information and Library Network (INFLIBNET) Centre is an autonomous Inter-University Centre of the UGC of India. It is a major National Programme initiated by the UGC in 1991 with its Head Quarters at Gujarat University Campus, Ahmedabad. Initially started as a project under the IUCAA, it became an independent Inter-University Centre in 1966. (http://www.inflibnet.ac.in.)

Its objectives are: (Chakravarty, and Singh, 2005)

- To promote and establish communication facilities to improve capability in information transfer and access, that provides support to scholarship, learning, research and academic pursuit through cooperation and involvement of agencies concerned.
- To establish INFLIBNET: Information and Library Network a computer communication network for linking libraries and information centers in universities, deemed to be universities, colleges,UGC information centers, institutions of national

importance and R&D institutions, etc. avoiding duplication of efforts.

INFLIBNET performs following major activities :(Bavakutty, and Azeez, 2006)

- Provides grants to universities to automate the libraries, establishing the network facilities and create an information technology environment.
- Developed and distributed Software for University Libraries (SOUL) which is integrated user friendly library management software. The latest version of the software is 2.0 which is competent to operate with the latest technologies and international standards such as MARC21, Unicode based and NCIP 2.0 based protocols for electronic surveillance and control.
- Indian Catalogue of University Libraries in India (IndCat) is Online Library Catalogue of books, theses and journals available in major university libraries in India which provides bibliographic description, location of the material in all subjects available in more than 112 university libraries. Thus, IndCat has over 10 million bibliographical records of books from more than 113 universities. In addition, the database of theses, expert databases, project databases and SEWAKOFFLINE database access facilities are also extended to the libraries of higher learning institutions.
- To enhance the skills of university library staff for implementation of INFLIBNET programme, it conducts training programme for library staff, onsite training for member library staff, training on SOUL software, holding CALIBER convention every year and workshops for senior level staff of the university libraries are conducted.
- It has brought out a document entitled 'INFLIBNET Standards and Guideline for Data Capturing 'prepared by a task force of experts based on Common Communication Format (CCF).

Another very important and significant landmark in the history of higher education and development of libraries in India is the establishment of "UGCINFONET DIGITAL LIBRARY CONSORTIUM" by the UGC on the concluding day of its Golden jubilee celebrations by his Excellency the then President of India, Dr. A.P.J Abdul Kalam at Vigyan Bhawan on28th December 2003.

UGC-INFONET is an innovative project launched by UGC to facilitate scholarly e-resources to Indian academies through joint partnership of UGC, INFLIBNET and ERNET. This includes interlinking of universities and colleges in the country electronically with a view to achieve maximum efficiency through Internet enabled teaching, learning and governance. The UGC-Infonet is overlaid on ERNET infrastructure in a manner so as to provide assured quality of service and optimum utilization of bandwidth resources. The network will be run and managed by ERNET India. The project is funded by UGC with 100 per cent capital investment and up to 90 per cent of recurring costs.UGC and ERNET India have signed the necessary MoU for this purpose. A joint technical and tariff committee, has been setup to guide and monitor the design, implementation and operations of UGCINFONET. Information for Library Network (INFLIBNET) an autonomous Inter-University Centre of UGC is the nodal agency for coordination and facilitation of the linkage between ERNET and the Universities. Under this programme, information and communication technologies (ICT) and internet will be used to transform learning environment from a monodimensional one to a multidimensional one. (Chakravarty). This was created to help and benefit more than 310 universities and about 14,000 colleges affiliated with these universities and approximately 10million students with the e-journals, thus, is a boon to higher education system in many ways.(http://www.inflibnet.ac.in/UGC-InfoNet/ugcinfonet.html#5).

UNIVERSITY LIBRARIES IN THE NEW MILLENNIUM

Keeping in view of the ever increasing significance of higher education for economic development, sound progress and political democracy, India embarked upon bringing about blue print on National Knowledge Commission in the year 2006. The National knowledge Commission has basically underscored the importance of expansion of education in terms of creating many more universities, transforming the system of regulation for higher education, enhancing public spending and diversifying sources of financing besides recommendations for fifty national universities. The Commission categorically emphasized the quality of education in terms of excellence by referencing existing universities, restructuring under-graduate college education and promoting enhanced quality of higher education system. In order to bring about qualitative change in library's functioning the National Knowledge Commission has recommended institution of National Mission on Library and Information Services (NMLIS), modernizing library management and introducing private and personal collections.[43]

CONCLUSION

In a university's education primary objective is to cater to the needs of students interested in higher education. A university mainly stands for higher learning and research where scholar and faculty members are head, students are the body and the library is the heart. A library is a centre where collection of documents is done to promote their use and also to facilitate information dissemination. The fundamental role of the library is to impart education and to support and promote the teaching needs of the faculty, research, extension and publication programmes.

The Radhakrishnan Commission (1948) concentrated on both philosophical and practical aspect of higher education and endorsed the view and vehemently supported university library. The Kothari Commission (1964-66) analyzed the Indian Education system and spelt functions of higher learning and streamlining the functions of a university library.

The significance of a library in a modern university was also upheld by Salder's University Commission (1917-19). UGC Library Committee (1957) headed by Dr. S. R. Ranaganathan advised it on matters relating to proper functioning and management of college and university libraries. The UGC accepted most of the recommendations of this committee. The UGC took special interest in university libraries and with the help of its Library Committee and its recommendations related to space, staff, equipments, collection development, services and establishment of INFLIBNET for the networking of university and the institutions of higher education and learning and the establishment of UGC-INFONET Digital Library Consortia.

The National Knowledge Commission (NKC) which came into being in 2006 made recommendations for institutions National Mission on library and Information Services (NMLIS) for creating, disseminating, optimally utilizing and preserving knowledge. The Knowledge Commission also laid stress upon modernizing library management, efficient and effective staffing of libraries and private and personal collections

REFERENCES

1. Prasher, R.G (1991), *Managing University Libraries*, Today and Tomorrow's Pub., New Delhi, p27.
2. Sewa Singh (1986), *Reference Services In Academic Libraries in India*, Ess Ess Pub, New Delhi, p.9.
3. Sankalia, H. D., (1972), *The University of Nalanda*, 2nd Rev. ed., Oriental Pub., Delhi, pp.72-73.
4. Mookerji, Radha Kumud (1969), *Ancient Indian Education*, 4th ed., Motilal Banarsidas, Delhi, p. 574.
5. Barua, Dipak Kumar (1964), "Nalanda University

Library", *Herald of Library Science*, Vol. 3 No.2-3, pp. 206-208.

6. Chakravorty, S.N. (1954), "Libraries in Ancient Times with Special Reference to India", *Indian Librarian*, Vol.9, No.2, Sept, p. 53.

7. Chinese Monk Fahien Who Visited India from 405 To 411 A.D. quote in Prasher, R.G (1991), *Managing University Libraries*, Today and Tomorrow's Pub., New Delhi, p. 27

8. Dutta, Bimal Kumar (1970), *Libraries and Librarianship of Ancient and Medieval India*, Atma Ram, Delhi, pp. 29-33.

9. Datta (1970), Ibid. p. 30.

10. Datta (1970), Ibid. p. 52.

11. Sewa Singh (1986), Op.cit. p. 11.

12. Datta (1970), Op.cit. p. 63

13. Narendra Nath Law (1973), *Promotion of Learning in India during Momammdan Rule*, Idarah-i-Adabiyat-i-Delhi, Delhi (Reprint), p. 151.

14. Prasher, R. G. (1991), Op.cit., p. 27.

15. Ibid. p. 28.

16. Ibid.

17. Ibid.

18. Ibid.

19. Indian University Commission, 1902 (1903), *Report*, Similar Central Printing Office, Simla, p. 13.

20. Indian University Commission, Ibid. p. 59.

21. India, Calcutta University Commission, 1917-1919, (1919), *Report of the Committee appointed by the Government of India to Enquire into Conditions and Prospects of the Calcutta University*, HMSO, London, Vol.1, p. 407.

22. Ibid.

23. Vishwanathan, C. G. (1972), *University Library of India : Principle and Policy*, New Delhi, pp. 6-7.

24. S. Bashruddin (1975), "The University Library its Functions and Problems", *ILA Bulletin*, Vol. 11 No. 1-2 p. 47.

25. Vishwanathan, C. G. (1972), Op.cit. p. 70.

26. Vishwanathan, C. G. (1957), "A Hundred Years of Indian University Libraries, 1876-1956: A Historical and Critical Survey", *Library Association Record*, Vol. 59, pp. 393-396.

27. Ibid.

28. Bose, P. C. (1963), "The Story of a Century Old University Library", *Library Herald*, Vol. 6 No. 2-3, p. 122.

29. Ranganathan, S. R. (1967), "Vitalising the education of University Libraries", in N. N. Gidwani (Ed.), *University libraries Then and Now*, First Seminar of University Libraries in India, held at Rajasthan University, Jaipur, 16-19, p. 66.

30. Ranganathan, S. R. (1963), "University Libraries Then and Now", Library Herald, Vol. 6 No. 2-3, p. 66.

31. Ibid.

32. Banerjee, P. K. (1964), "Reflections of the University Libraries in India", *Indian Librarian*, Vol. 19 No. 1, pp. 23-27.

33. Indian University Education Commission, 1948-49 (1951), *Report*, Manager of Publication, New Delhi, 2 Vols. Chairman S. Radhakrishan, p. 110.

34. Bhargava, G. D. (1959), "University Libraries an Educational Set up of India", *Indian Librarian*, Vol. 14 No. 3, p. 117.

35. Samuels, Mathai (1964-65), "University Grants

Commission Retrospect", *Journal University Education*, Vol. 3, pp. 175-180.

36. India UGC (1965), *Report of the Library Committee*, UGC, New Delhi.

37. India UGC (1965), Ibid. p. 228.

38. Ibid. pp. 141-50.

39. Indian Education Commission 1964-66 (1966), *Report*, Manager of Publication, Delhi pp. 519-523.

40. Ibid. p. 71.

41. Jugal Kishore (1981), *Personal Management in Libraries*, Ess Ess, Pub., New Delhi, p. 27.

42. Ibid.

43. Knowledge Commission, available at http://knowledgecommission.gov.in/recommendations (Accessed Sept. 1, 2008)

2

Collection Development: Its Organization and Services

The primary purpose of libraries is to preserve knowledge which is available in any documentary form. However, the scope has widened to ensure that the user is satisfied by using it. University libraries acquire the documents to provide them with information to satisfy the changing needs of the students, faculty and researchers. The objective of the academic libraries has been subject to transformation from preservation to provision of information to utmost satisfaction of the user. The term "Collection Development" (CD) has been evolved to emphasize personalized services to satisfy user's demand.[1]

Collection Development encompasses all plans formulated for the systematic and rational building of a collection. The term includes a group of activities i.e., assessing the user needs, evaluating the present collection, determining selection policy, coordinating the choice of items, re-evaluating and storing parts of the collection, and planning for resource sharing.[2] A collection development policy involves selection and acquisition (procurement) of library materials to meet both present as well as future requirements of users which is constrained by limited financial resources, diversity of user information needs and availability of vast sources of information.[3] The topic 'Collection Development' is a planning and decision making process that covers-broad range of activities related to the policies and procedures of selection, assessment of user needs, evaluating present collection, weeding out, and storing parts of the collection and planning for resource sharing.[4]

COLLECTION DEVELOPMENT: A CONCEPT

A collection development is a process which permits the library to develop a collection of materials responding to the information needs and service requirements of the users. It has also been defined "as a process that allows for the identification of the strengths and weaknesses of the documents collection of a library in terms of the needs of the users and the resources of the community. It is a universal process in the library world in which the library professional assembles a variety of materials in order to satisfy the demands of the users. This dynamic and constant cycle brings together six elements: user study, policies, selection, acquisition, weeding and evaluation".[5] Sanchez defines collection development as a process which assumes that the information needs of the users are satisfied in an economic fashion and inside of a reasonable period of time using resources as much internal as external to the organization.[6]

Collection development can be divided into two parts; such as, "Basic functions" and "Umbrella function". They are briefly described as below:

The Basic-functions are performed by all academic libraries development process, i.e., selection of library materials, acquisitions donations, weeding, preservation, and intellectual freedom, and the Umbrella functions are performed to inform library staff of the constituents of collection development process itself, i.e., Collection

Development Policies, Users Needs Assessment, and Collection Assessment. Though these are not necessarily performed by all academic libraries, however these are vital tools of collection development. [7]

According to Evans[8] collection development consists of community. It is the group of people who use the services of the library and may be a political unit (a country, a state, or a municipality) or it may be an entity more specialized (such as university, a school, a research center, a firm) collection development therefore includes analysis of Community, Collection Policies, Selection Policies, Acquisitions, discarding Policies and evaluation of collection.

FACTORS AFFECTING COLLECTION DEVELOPMENT

Aims and objectives of the parent institution is the basis for framing priorities of collection development. For example, library's objective is to contribute' to maximize the organization's profits if the aim of its parent organization is related to profit. Collection development is a continuous process and it requires utmost attention on the part of the policy makers. Some of the important factors should be kept in mind while formulating collection development policy, viz., i) Philosophy of the Organization; ii) Nature of the community; iii) High standards of intellectual contents; iv) Relevance of contents; v) Cooperation and networking; vi) Access vs. ownership; vii) Relationship with other information service units; viii) Availability of budget and existing reasons; and ix) Revision of policy.[9]

PREREQUISITES OF COLLECTION DEVELOPMENT

Collection development is interplay of the libraries aims and strategies of the librarian and, his staff in order to meet the user's requirement and, for its implementation; a clear policy of acquisition, periodic evaluation of the collection and the systematic weeding out of documents.

According to Bloomfield[10] observed that the collection

development involves identification of some of the key issues such as:

(a) Identification of the purpose and mission of the library / parent organization,(b)The library staff or a committcc formulates the library's collection development policy,(c)Matching between users' requirements and institution's aim and objectives,(d)Budgetary provisions and the contingent problems,(e)Working out the strategies for implementing the policies and programmes, and(f)Policy statements have to be maintained, revised and updated.

Collection development is thus a dynamic and continuous ac-tivity, which involves the users, the library staff, and the subject experts on selection team. It is a process to develop a need-based, up-to-date, and balanced collection which is sufficient to meet the docu-ment and information needs of the users.[11]

Collection development in other words is a powerful audit aspect of a library, its use is enhanced by efficient organization of the collection, accessibility to it, circulation of the docu-ments, and maintenance of the collection. Element of objectivity has been introduced in collection development process with the development of quantitative techniques and other parameters for usage of documents. Ranganathan's First Law of Library Science; *Books are for use,* is however, a seminal guide for this purpose.[12]

USERS OF LIBRARIES

The collection-building activities are designed in respect of the users to be catered. Since an academic library is to support the teaching, research and extension programmes of its organization, its collection and services are to cater to the curricular, co-curricular needs of the students, faculty, and research scholars and background material by the undergraduate and post-graduate students as well as research scholars.[13]

Information needs of a user depend on different of factors, discipline and activities. According to Voigt[14] three types of users' information needs or ap-proaches are recognized, viz. (i) Current approach, (ii) Everyday approach, (iii) Exhaus-tive approach. The fourth approach was added by Grogan (1982) i.e., the browsing approach. And more recently, one more approach has been added. It is a catching-up approach.[15]c

Current approach which user makes an attempt to get the new views and ideas from existing concepts. Everyday approach is to meet the frequent information needs of the user during the course of his research investigation. Through Exhaustive approach, user makes an attempt to obtain almost all the available information regarding the concerned problem.[16]In the browsing approach the user seeks information on the areas of knowledge which is outside his specialized field. The catching-up approach relates to obtaining information that provides a broad overview about the problem. It involves procuring complete information briefly and quickly.[17]

COLLECTION DEVELOPMENT POLICY

A plan is required in every library which ensures efficient collection development by identifying and correcting collection weaknesses while maintaining its strengths. A collection development policy statement is a document that represents a plan of action and informa-tion which is used to guide the staffs' thinking and decision making. The staff specifically consults the collection development policy while considering which sub-ject areas is to be augmented and thus determine how much emphasis is to be given to each area. The policy should be such that it must seem to be a means of communication with library's service population and the people who provide its funding.[18]

Policy guidelines are vital for a need based, balanced and up-to-date collection. Without a policy adhocism and confusion might prevail and adhering to the policy would minimize bias and thus a quality collection is en-sured. As collection development is a continuous and never-ending ac-tivity, a well-thought out long term policy is needed which should provide an answer to the following.[19]

1. Who has the responsibility for seeing that a policy is setup and regularly implemented?
2. Who should have final authority for directing and controlling the distribution of book funds?
3. What material should be acquired?
4. Who should participate in the selection?"

According to Evans[20] (1987), a policy document should have (i)a brief general description of the community to be served;(ii)identification of specific clientele to be served;(iii)a general Statement regarding the parameters of collection, such as specific subject field and type of formats that the library will acquire;(iv)the statement on general limitations and priorities that will determine how the collection will be developed, and(v)keeping in mind the library's role in cooperative collection development and networking; the policy should make it clear as to whether the basic philosophy is self-sufficiency or cooperation.

Besides this Perkins (1997), "made certain recommendations of clients and knowledge of their information needs which are the key elements in deciding what to buy."[21]

While deciding the areas of the policy, the policy writers classify the col-lections into constituent subject areas, identify types of material collected, and specify the primary user group for each subject. Collection development officers have to collect, analyze and evaluate data relating to consumer needs. Collection of data is followed by assigning priorities to each area, perhaps by format within each area. All of this is done with the goal of achieving a proper balance of subjects and supplying the information needs of the service community.[22]

The next part of the policy is a very vital one and it involves fixing responsibility for the development of the collection. In a small library, the task is done by the librarian himself, while in case of a large-scale library the task is delegated to the staff. However, the ultimate responsibility would lie with the chief librarian. Also, the policy should itself be clear as to on what basis the selectors would take decisions. A review policy for evaluating the performance of selections should also be formulated.[23]

The collection development policy statement must also deal with gifts; deselection and discards of documents, their evaluation, complaints and censorship. Though each and every topic is individually significant and important and separate policy statement can be prepared for each one and this is usually not done. A gist of or summary of these topics is prepared by the collection policy writers instead.[24]

There is also A need for an overview section that defines terms and outlines the context of the policy. What does the policy cover? Does it include one-time purchases of CD-ROM products, only ongoing subscription services, or both? Does it cover the library's linking to various websites?[25]

Having the policy prepared with considerable efforts of the staff, the next step involves getting it approved by the appropriate authorities such as the governing board so that everyone agrees in principle in order to serve the user's community.[26]There should also be periodic renewal and revision of policy to keep up with changes in users' need and to make sure that it reflects current practices and procedures in the libraries.

SELECTION OF READING MATERIAL

The term 'library material' spans across a wide variety of items ranging from the printed book to the micro forms and non-print forms like the sound recordings and motion pictures. The non-print material and the printed books are same as regards their usefulness as information sources.[27] Selection is the heart of the collection development process and it aims to build the library's resources for a particular user community. Skill, knowledge, and the right tools are required to select appropriate library materials that meet the needs of the community. It is a challenge to build a balanced collection that meets the needs of user community.[28]

BOOK SELECTION

In a study in the year 1980 Katz had identified that about 5, 00,000 books were published every year and more than 1,00,000 of them were in English. About 65,000 to 1,00,000 periodicals were publish-ed which now would be much more than two folds making it impossible for any university library to purchase all the titles due to the limited financial resources. The book selection, hence should comply with the basic principles of book selection, viz., McColvin's 'Demand Theory', Dewey's 'Best book to the largest number of the readers at the least cost', and Drury's 'Right book to the Right reader at the Right time'.[29]

For book selection, knowledge of the subject is primary requirement. McGril and Hickey (1984), feel that book selection has to be done by bibliographers, reference librarians, departmental librarians, faculty members and combination of various other groups. No single librarian or faculty should be made respon-sible for the selection. Interaction with readers, handling their Information requirements and subject background provides an opportunity to library staff in proper selection. Documentary needs of students and researchers should be known to the faculty.[30]

According to Nazir Ahmed (1984), materials are selected by the library staff with the aid and advice of academic staff. In practice, the staff members take little interest in advancing their suggestions for additions to the stack.[31]

Francis Drury in the year 1930[32] clearly stated certain basic principles which govern the selection of reusing material for a library. It states: "To provide the right book to the right reader at the right time". In this statement the reader is the central theme and the veracity of documents is in relation to the readers and the material/document should be available to the reader.

In the year 1925 L. R. McColvin[33] advanced his Demand and Supply Theory of Book Selection where in he sates, "Books in themselves are nothing. They have no more meaning than the white paper upon which they are printed, until they are made serviceable by demand. The more closely book selection is related to demand, the greater is the resultant and possible service.

Melvil Dewey's principle states: "The best reading for the largest number at the least cost"[34] According to this principle a library should select the best available documents that satisfy the users within the limited financial resources. The term 'best' is relative. It means a document 'which "may be the best in its own field, the best that will be read, the best of which good use will be made, the best that will answer a certain demand". The best Documents which satisfy the just demands of the users for recreation, knowledge and study; social and cultural needs of the users are regarded as best: A classic or a master-piece may not be in demand for the time being, but it is the best book to be selected for its literary worth and future purposes.

FIVE LAWS OF LIBRARY SCIENCE AND DOCUMENT SELECTION[35]

Dr. S.R. Ranganathan's first three Laws of Library Science are helpful in for-mulating the principles of document selection.

The first law emphasizes that only those documents should be selected which satisfies the clients. While selecting the documents, the present and potential requirements of the users must be kept in view. A school or public library should avoid the selection of expensive books which are not likely to be in frequent demand. For a childrens library, the books should be profusely illustrated, printed in bold typeface and must also be attractive. The second law of library science—

every reader his/her document -directs— the book selector to select documents in order to cater for the informational needs of all the users of the library. The subject or the language or the style of exposition of documents to be selected should be in accordance with the requirement of all categories of the users. Adequate knowledge of the users' documents is necessary for document selection. The third law of library science— every book/document its reader— suggests that all efforts should be made to put to use each and every document of value which have been selected in anticipation of the needs of the users. If compliance of the first two laws of library science are kept in mind it would ensure that the selection of documents and development of collection is on the right tracks.

Selection Policy enables a library to achieve quality, objectivity and consistency in the process of document selection and thus ensures that resources satisfy the information needs of the customers. Some libraries have separate selection and acquisition policies, while others put selection policy as a part of acquisition policy. Selection policy may include the aspects such as[36] (i) *Core Collection:* It includes resources that are critical for fulfilling the objectives of the parent body and thus receive the highest priority. (ii) *Supporting Collection:* Includes items that supplement the core collection, providing additional information and adding value to the functioning of the organization. (iii) *Peripheral Collection:* Selection of core and supporting collections receive first and second priority respectively and peripheral collection is selected on the basis of budget availability. They consist of costly online services that are rarely used, fringe publications that do not form part of basic needs of the users, and the items that can be obtained from other libraries on inter-library loan. (iv) *Kinds of Resources:* Library's policy must include specific guidelines for selecting different kinds of resources, such as general books, reference sources (such as dictionaries, encyclopedias, yearbooks, directories), serials, reports (both internal and external), online services, electronic resources, grey literature. (v) *Formats:* All formats should be considered. (vi) *Online Sources:* Access to online databases should be provided. (vii) Inter-library loan and document delivery. *(viii) Project-bused Products and Service:* There may be a need for the purchase of information resources beyond the scope of resources covered under the laid down selection policy to support the ongoing research projects within the parent organization.

According to Drury, [37] "A necessary part of selection process is the choosing titles from many valuable aids". Selection of books is done through various tools like catalogues, leaflets (both print and electronic formats), journals, magazines, web sites, online services, CD ROMs. Many publishers bring out catalogues covering resources prior to their publication. Current reviews, National bibliographies, Trade bibliographies, Subject bibliographies, best books recommended lists and core collections of important libraries help the selectors to a large extent.

Document selection policies have been replaced by material selection policies due to the increasing production of non-print materials which cannot be ignored. With the increasing emphasis on non-traditional sources of information, librarians must content themselves with formats other than books. This material range from other than print media such as newspapers, periodicals and pamphlets or ephemeral collections to non-print formats like tapes, motion pictures and so on. The librarian needs to be aware of the multitude of communication formats available and also to be more knowledgeable and skilled to be able to make intelligent decisions regarding their unique contribution to the library goals by providing appropriate information to its patrons.[38]

Now a days, several information resources are available in electronic format such as CD ROMs; online sources via web or dial-up access as well as in print format (hard copy). The same resources in multiple formats should be purchased only if they satisfy the needs of different user groups and have an advantage in searching the data base as cost is a constraint. A decision to purchase a particular format by considering either a change over from print to electronic format, or changing from CD ROM to online must be based on the certain considerations such as(i) Availability of Technical Infrastructure which comprises existing networks, intranets, internet, telephone communication, capacity of computers, etc, that affects the quality of electronic delivery of information. In the absence of any good infrastructure, interests of the user seeking information will suffer. In most of developing countries, telephone communication and computer networks are of poor quality, and due to the shortage of electricity and frequent power failures, there are often breakdowns in the computer systems which require backup services in the form of electricity generators. In this regard the use of Uninterrupted Power Supply (UPS) is of paramount significance which ensures that the unsaved data are not wiped out due to sudden power cuts.(ii) Different versions of a document may have varying contents regarding scope, updating, indexing, referencing, illustrations, etc. which may be significant or insignificant.

(iii) Cost of material purchased varies depending on the time of the year when purchases are made, for e.g. CD ROMS are cheaper when comparing the cost with print formats. (iv) The Size of the library budget often becomes a constraint. A library may prefer a particular resource due to a large price difference between two or more available resources. (v) User Behavior is another significant factor. The ability to use information technology varies from user to user. Some may not have such abilities while others may have adequate expertise. (vi) The vendors sometimes offer a package deal. While purchasing one title in electronic format, one may be required to purchase a package consisting of a group of titles (especially while subscribing serials) including the one needed by the library. There are also vendors who insist the library to purchase both print and electronic versions. A library may then have no alternative. (vii) Before going for e-documents one should find out (a) what are the conditions of licensing regarding access, copying and distribution? (b) What technical infrastructure is required? (c) Is the access for electronic serials subscribed and paid for all time, even though the library may stop subscribing to it in future at a later stage? (d) What is the retrospective coverage for the serials? (e) How long the vendor will provide access to electronic books?(viii) Changing from printed resources to electronic resources involve changes in workflows and procedures which may be easy to learn and adapt for the younger members of the staff but other may stiffly oppose it.[39]

Furthermore the rising cost and decline in purchasing power of individual libraries makes it difficult to acquire the electronic resources and this has led to collaborative selection of these information resources. For this purpose, they form into an unofficial consortium where one library in the group purchases a particular item and the cost is shared across the group. While making the payment of subscription an additional charge need to be paid, a user license is obtained from the vendor, allowing users of each library belonging to the consortium to have access and user rights. Each library may select a different resource, paying subscription plus additional charges, and offering access to the other libraries also in the consortium on reciprocal access.[40]

ACQUISITION OF RESOURCES

According to Gelfand[41] acquisition programme is a plan for carrying out the objectives of the library with respect to the development of collection. It should be a long-range plan, flexible in nature and subject to periodic review and revision. The plan should be started for a period of five years or more with the approval and support of the authorities within the budget. For obtaining support and co-operation of the faculty and library staff, wide publicity should be given to the programme. Gelfand further quotes Wilson and Swank who describe the acquisition *as* "the continuous systematic-analysis of weak spots in the book collection through the checking of bibliographies against the library's holdings, the submission to the faculty lists of materials not owned, the rating by the faculty and library staff of these titles, and finally the preparation of want or desiderata lists". The lists then go to the order department where the process of procurement begins. Acquisition departments also have some internal goals,[42] such as; quick procurement of orders; ensuring lowest possible unit cost by keeping work processes simple; to keep work processes simple; to achieve the lowest possible unit cost; and , to develop close and friendly working relationships with other library units and with vendors.

Collection analysis is the best basis for evaluation. According to Katz, the purpose of analysis and evaluation of the collec-tion is to determine the quality of the collection. Evaluating such large collections is a difficult task. Evaluation can be done either by analyzing how well each individual item is and how good the item suits the particular needs of the users. To evaluate in these two terms utilization of the user's knowledge is essential.Katz[43] further gave the possible ways of evaluation. They are: (i) Statistics on holdings, use and expenditures; (ii) *Checking* lists, catalogues, bibliographies, etc.; (iii) Obtaining opinions from regular users ;(iv) Examining the collection directly and applying standards; and (v)Testing document delivery capability.

According to him the library can cut 80% of book collection and 40% to 60% of periodicals, but still can serve 99% of the users.

Good collection need not necessarily guarantee good utilization of documents. Modification of the existing acquisition policy through evaluation would certainly improve the quality of the collection.

ORGANIZATION OF THE COLLECTION

The collection should be orchestrated in order to superlative repossession of information and materials. The two technical processes cataloging and classification will mirror nationally rectified matter of forms in sync with other academic libraries. Cataloging and classification have been synthesized owing to the fact that these are twin processes that make certain systematic design for the materials in a library. Conventionally classification guarantees the helpful marshalling of books and documents on the shelves of the library. cataloging, as far back as 1876 itself Charles Ami Cutter[44] has put it in the following manner:

1. To enable a person to find a book of which either:
   a. the author, or
   b. the title, or
   c. the subject is known
2. To show what the library has
   a. by a given author
   b. on a given subject
   c. in a given kind of literature
3. To assist in the choice of a book
   a. as to its edition (bibliographically)
   b. as to its character (literary or topical)

The conventional schemes of classification have been unreliable, known as "logical absurdly" as advocated by Trevons[45] and the same has been consented by J.H. Shera[46] on the basis that classification schemes intend to limit the multi dimensional knowledge to a unidimensional order, thereby introducing the linear arrangement on the shelves of the library. This, per se, impairs the usage of classification as an efficient way for arrangement of documents in a library. Thus, one has to mostly rely on the library catalogues which have better edge on classification, as one can embrace multiple entry system for a single document and fulfill different and multi dimensional modes of the user.[47]

Materials should be catalogued and classified in a planned manner to make them ready as soon as possible after their receipt in the library. Materials to be catalogued constitute print, non-print and electronic resources and the remote-data bases for which the library is subscribing. In the modern era, , we have the following general schemes of classification the world over.

1. Melvil Dewey's Decimal Classification(DDC)
2. Charles Ami Cutter's Expansive Classification(EC)
3. Library of Congress Classification(LCC)
4. J. D. Brown's Subject Classification(SC)
5. Universal Decimal Classification(UDC)
6. S. R. Ranganathan's Colon Classification(CC)
7. Henery Evelyn Bliss's Bibliographic Classification(BC)
8. F. Riders International Classification(IC)

Similarly for the process of cataloging, there are numerous cataloguing codes available.

1. C.A.Cutter's Rules for Dictionary Catalogue
2. Anglo American Cataloging Rule(AACR)
3. S.R. Ranganathan, s, Classified Catalogue Code(CCC)

ON-LINE PUBLIC ACCESS CATALOGUE (OPAC)

As that of the traditional cataloguesOPAC also covers all the bibliographic information of the collected documents in the library and it provides an access to library collection. It has great utility in the organization and dissemination of the collection. OPAC is latest and a very flexible catalogue, providing instantaneous and sophisticated entry to any recorded information with the help of a computer. ALA Glossary defines OPAC as, "A computer based and supported library catalogue (bibliographic database) designed to be accessed via terminals so that library users may directly and efficiently search for and retrieve bibliographic records within the assistance of a human intermediary such as a specially trained member of the library staff.[48] In OPAC, users have facilities of interacting with catalogues, modify search methods and information is displayed so as to maximize search results, based on the own information needs of the users. The OPAC user has paramount significance as it has the capacity even to influencing the relationships between OPAC and its users.

LIBRARY SERVICES

As the libraries are service providers and the university library is no exception to it. University library is considered as a spring of knowledge and information provided will always be valued at a premium. In the modern significantly and socially vigilant society, especially when the grains of right to information are gaining much currency, the university libraries are expected to be more responsive and interactive with their users.The library service which brings the staff in direct contact with the users in order to provide the right information at the right time and also to help them in the finding out resources and thus providing required information should be given due emphasizes.

The libraries offer various kinds of services viz.,

CIRCULATION OPERATION

One of the prime functions of a university library is the circulation of documents which is popularly known as lending of library materials. Every library performs it and intends to satisfy its users. Helen Geer[49] has advocated that while embarking on a circulation system for a library it should be evaluated on the parameter of cost involved in its organization and administration, improvement in reader's services and reduction in costly records.

The following systems are being widely adopted in the world of librarianship from the very beginning till dates by different libraries. They are(i) Ledger system; (ii)Permanent slip or card system; (iii) Browne charging system; (iv) Newark charging system; (iv) Detriot charging system; (v) Token charging system; (vi) Photographic charging system; (vii) Audio-charging system; (viii) Visual-record charging system; (ix) Tab charging system; (x) Double call slip charging system; and (xi) Computer-based charging system.

REFERENCE SERVICE

According to Dr. S.R. Ranganathan, reference service

is right contact means, contact between the right reader and the right book at the right time and in the right personal way. "He is of the view that the establishment of such a contact is "the only available and effective method"[50] of discharging the function of converting the users into habitual users. Thus, he adds that "Reference service is the establishing of contact between reader and book by personal service.[51] In reference service the emphasis is laid on personal service to each and every user and thus helps him in finding documents. Samuel Rothstein similarly defines it as "personal assistance given by the librarian to the individual reader in pursuit of information".[52] According to Margaret Hutchins, "Reference work includes the direct, personal aid within a library to persons in search of information for what ever purpose, and also various library activities especially aimed at making information as easily available as possible.[53] A university library is supposed to perform the following functions such as teaching, research, publication, conservation of knowledge and ideas, extension and service, and interpretation.[54] A university library is a sub-set of a university establishment. Thus, it exists to achieve the objectives of its parent organization. In other words a university library should intend to spur up the function. The clientele mainly consists of students, teachers and research scholars. The requirement of the users is diverse and varies. The reference services provided in the university libraries include the following:[55]

i. Instruction in the use of the library,

ii. Provision of general and specific information,

iii. Assistance in the location (or searching) of documents or use of library catalogue understanding of reference books,

iv. Literature search,

v. Reader's advisory service,

vi. Compilation of bibliographies, preparation of indexing and abstracting service.

vii. Reservation of documents: In case a document has not

been loaned, then a user who needs it can get it reserved, so that when the document is returned then the user can be informed and he can get it issued.

viii. Inter library loan: Inter-library loan refers to request for a document not available in the library. Whatever might be the nature of a library, but it should take advantage of borrowing books from other libraries.

ix. Holding of library exhibitions including display of new additions to the library,

x. Maintenance of clippings, and

xi. Maintenance of vertical files containing pamphlets like prospectuses, report? etc.

The kind and nature of reference services to be provided in the libraries will on the curricula, research programs, methodology of teaching and objectives of university education.

INFORMATION SERVICE

Apart from reference services, libraries need to provide information and bibliographic services. The term information service has a wide ambit and is not restricted to a specific item of information provided on demand but also the provision of information in anticipation. There are numerous modes to forecast and predict the actual demands of the users. Users approach to seeking information may cover bulletins, bibliographies, documentation lists, document delivery, annual reports, literature surveys, CAS, SDI, On-line searching, reports, etc.[56]

Information service is the prime activity in any kind of library. In university library particularly, it is indispensable for researchers as well as faculty members and the students.

BIBLIOGRAPHIC SERVICE

Bibliography, today indicate a gamut of documents but mainly material arranged in a logical way to fulfill the needs on demands of users. According to the Oxford English Dictionary bibliography as the systematic description and history of books, their authorship, printing, publishing, editions, etc. Andale Esdaile states the bibliography was the art of recording books, and the science of making of books and their extant record.[57] The usual attribute of these descriptions is that bibliographies list books in a systematic way to reveal the source of knowledge. The scope of marshalling of bibliographic records has been widened with the application of information technology. A bibliography is reduced by numerous limitations so as to restrict its size to a handy book form. There are no such constraints for electronic storage of bibliographic records. A bibliography may cover only a few thousand citations of books, but a database provides for unlimited scope. These are known to cover millions of such records and are updated at regular intervals; computers have assisted in compilation of bibliographic data through its transfer to electronic storage.[58]

The bibliographies are distinguished by their character and in function. There are various types of bibliographies available to fulfill the needs of their users, viz., (i)Subject Bibliography (ii)Historical Bibliography(iii)Descriptive Bibliography(iv)Comprehensive Bibliography(v)Universal Bibliography, etc. -

ABSTRACTING SERVICE

The modern era is characterized as an era of information age. There is no single branch of knowledge where so much of quantum of information is not being generated. Therefore, huge sources of information are documented, but it creates problem of not only in organizing the knowledge but also in the selection of quality and important information products. An abstracting service intends to facilitate the summarization of new documents and inform the users about the topical areas of interest to them.[59] The various kinds of abstracts are recognized by their scope on coverage. The commonly known abstracts are indicative and informative. Other kinds of abstracts are author abstract, locative abstract, telegraphic abstract, auto abstract and, so on.

INDEXING SERVICE

Another important service necessitated in libraries is indexing service. With the escalation in quantity and complexity of published literature, and with the awakening that information is of paramount significance for research, socio-economic development and decision-making, the utility of an index has garnered wide acceptance. Sizeable improvement in quality and design of an index has been made to match the varied requirements of the users and in tandem act as a forceful communication link between the sources of information and the users of information[60].

An index is an organized tool to the text of any reading matter or to the contents of other collected documentary materials, covering a series of entries, with headings shaped in alphabetical or other chosen order, and with references to reveal where each item indexed are located. Thus, it is cogently perceived that an index is a list systematically arranged providing enough details about each item, so that it can be figured and brought out.[61]There are various types of indexes; such as (i)Book indexes;(ii)Indexes of collections; (iii)Periodical indexes;(iv)Newspapers indexes;(v)Citation indexes

CURRENT AWARENESS SERVICE (CAS)

The researchers, students and faculty members are required to be abreast of the latest development in their respective areas to remain updated and to sustain the challenges of fast-growing competitive environment. Pertinent current information is available in newsletters, newspapers, journals and other micro-documents.[62]

According to B. C.Vickery CAS as "more frequently and more adequately met by circulation than by retrieving current journals, newly received books and reports, abstract bulletins and the like being fed and scanned by users".[63] The

Librarians Glossary defines CAS as "a system, and often a publication, for notifying current documents to users of libraries and information services, e.g. selective dissemination services, bulletin, indexing service, current literature".[64]

SELECTIVE DISSEMINATION OF INFORMATION (SDI)

The term SDI was coined by Hans Peter Luhn for the first time in 1959. A service which is personal rather than common; it has evolved out of the development of key term indexes. Viewed as a 'Personalized CAS, SDI serves high interest areas. Luhn defines SDI as the service concerned with the channeling of new ideas of information from whatever source to those points within the organization where the probability of usefulness, in connection with current work of interest, is high.[65]

The SDI encapsulate a strategy to prepare users services manual and computerized methods are in operation mainly depending upon the level of automation of library services.

REPROGRAPHIC SERVICES

The term reprography was used for the first time in 1954 as a generic term for all kinds of facsimile reproduction of documents, covering in its scope, processes and techniques related with photo copying, micro copying, blue printing, electro coping, thermo copying dycline reproduction, etc. In earlier times, all these processes and technique were called a copying which without doubt was wider in is ambit and did encompass copy-typing and duplicating in the offices, photocopying in the libraries and blueprinting in drawing office.[66] According to H. Bose[67] reprographic service is a group of mechanical devices whereby one or multiple copies of a document can be made through copying and duplicating process. But reprography covers not only devices but processes and techniques and also includes mechanical along with photographic, thermal and electronic processes too.

Hawken's[68] definition is easy to appreciate. He states reprography as a term applied to draw attention to the copies of processes and methods applied for both copying and duplicating documents. The role of reprography is instrumental in communication. In the modern era, where there is proliferation of information, reprography facilities an information scientist to bring home to researcher, rightly at his desk, the literature pertinent to his area of subject from numerous sources.

TRANSLATION SERVICE

The development of nation hinges on the maximum usage of information within the length and breadth of country and outside. There are numerous languages which have documented the pace of progress and achievement in various arenas of knowledge. Western countries made significant scientific advances in the 20th century mainly in languages like English, German and French. In recent years, Japan has been acknowledged as bigwig in areas of economics and information. It is calculated that more than half of the global scientific and technical literature consist of 1.5 million items in languages other than English. A scientist prefers to use a document in his own language which will assist in applying it more conveniently. The way-out of the problem is to develop adequate infrastructure for getting the intended document-changed into a language familiar to the user. In university library milieu, this service is pertinent for researcher mainly for scientific research. [69]

CD-ROM (COMPUTER DISC-READ ONLY MEMORY) SERVICE

CD-ROM is one of the storage media developed due to information explosion has well as the urgency for quicker processing and accessing of information. CD-ROM is known to be a revolution in information media. CD-ROM technology has proven itself as blessing for libraries in facilitating library service to the users. CD-ROM is more accessible for searching the information and as, it occupies less space and has large storing capacity, it is more suited for university libraries.[70]

ON-LINE SERVICES

On-line system is also a revolution, in which the user is provided a seat at a terminal connected to database and has the capacity to interact with computer, shaping search strategy on the basis of response and the searcher has quick access to the database. The user can interrogate the computer directly. The output can be printed out or displayed on the screen. The computer acts as storage place for accumulation of information. Online indicate that users have access to information though the usage of video display and keyboard. The user can operate the keyboard, give the commands and the outcome can be revealed on video display or cathode ray tube. If the user read printed record then he has to push a button and record will be printed out. If the user has numerous indexes and abstracts available to search at a computer terminal, the contents of all those indexes and abstract is known as data-base. [71]

CONCLUSION

The collection development policy ensures active participation of the authorities, the users and the library staff in the activity of building a collection. It lays down collection goals of the library, and determines who has selection responsibility, and also the selection criteria, acquisition procedures including the process to handle the electronic resources. Thus collection development policy should be based on the aims and objectives of the library. Selection policy should be sound and comprehensive to build up an adequate collection of resources and it also ensures judicious spending of money for building resources to meet the information needs of the users and bring consistency to the process of selection of resources. The role of the librarian is becoming increasingly complex due to exponential growth of resources, the number of formats, delivery options and charges. The decrease in purchasing power of the currency further aggravates the problem.

The success of the process of the acquisition of documents requires knowledge of publishers and book trade and envisages an understanding of the ordering procedures, practices and policies, and also of policies regarding gifts and exchanges. The acquisition librarian should have a bibliographical flair to be able to detect cases of duplication either at the indent stage or at the stage of placing orders. Sending orders is a work of great responsibility and the librarian should scrutinize the orders carefully to detect errors, if any. In the present day environment, the vendor has to be dynamic in discharging his responsibility. Besides, performing the traditional role of buying the books, periodical publications and other materials, he has also to carry out the task of shelf preparation, distribution of e-books and e-journals, document delivery, etc. With the introduction of Internet, it has become possible to provide electronic resources to users directly at their desktops. The communication between librarians and vendors, and the process of seeking answers to queries, or sending orders has become fast. It has accelerated the process of acquisition. Services to the users of the library have significantly improved due to these developments.

The discipline of collection development is instrumental in the advancement of the organization of information. The quality of the collection is in tandem with service offered in any information institute or university depends on the proper selection and acquiring of the information sources. The pursuit of the collection development entails policies that guide its cardinal moments and garner procedures and necessary processing that assist the task of professional collection development in charge and assist them in decision-making. The information policies have to be refashioned to be in sync with the requirements of organization and facilitate information to all its members. In case of local area, it has to be physically attached with computer by cable. In case of a remote place, the terminal will connect via telephone line or via communication satellite.

REFERENCES

1. Laxman Rao,N., and Ratna Rao, N. (1993), "Collection Development in University Libraries", in, Issac, Dorothy, Raju, A.A.N. and Ramaiah (Ed.), *Academic Libraries Role in the National Development*, T.R. Pub, Madras.

2. Parmeswaran, M (1997), "Collection Development in University Libraries: Policy and Procedures", *DESIDOC Bulletin of Information Technology*, Vol.17 No.2, p.11.

2. Singh, S.P. and Krishna Kumar (2005), *Special Libraries in the Electronic Environment*, Bookwell, New Delhi, p.80.

3. Ravichandra Rao, I. K. (1997), "Impact of Recent Advances in Information Technology on Collection Development", *DESIDOC Bulletin of Information Technology*, Vol.17 No.1, p.3.

4. Evans, G. Edward (2004), *Developing Library and Information Centre Collections*, 4th ed., Libraries Unlimited, Greenwood Pub., Colorado, pp.16-17.

5. Sanchez Vignau, Susana, Barbara and Meneses, Grizly (2005), "Collection Development Policies in University Libraries : A Space Reflection", *Collection Building*, Vol. 24 No.1, p.36.

6. Available at http://www.lib.az us/cdt/coll dev.htm (Accessed 20th March, 2007)

7. Evans, G. Edward (1987), *Developing Library and Information Centre Collections*, Libraries Unlimited, Littleton, Colorado.

8. Singh, S.P. (2005), Op.cit. p. 80.

9. Bloomfield, B. C. (1987), "Collection Development the Key Issues" in S. Conall, (Ed.), *Collection Development Options For efficient Management*, Tayler Graham, London.

10. Prasher, R.G. (1993), *Developing Library Collections*, Medellian, New Delhi, p.15.

11. Ibid, p.16.

12. Ibid.

13. Voigt, M J. (1961), *Scientists Approaches to Information*, ALA, New York, pp.22-33.

14. Grogan quoted in Singh, S.P. (2005), Op.cit, p.80.

15. Voigt, M J. (1961), Op.cit, pp.22-33.

16. Singh, S.P. (2005), Op.cit, p.81.

17. Evans, G. Edward (2004), Op.cit, p.70.

18. Wilson, L.R and Tauber, M.F. (1956), *The University Library*, Coloumbia Press, New York, p.349.

19. Evans. G. Edward (1987), Op.cit, p.146.

20. Perkins L, Ed. (1979), *Guidelines for Collection Development*, American Library Association, p.20.

21. Evans, G.Edward (2004), Op.cit, p.76.

22. Evans, G.Edward (2004), Ibid, p.80.

23. Ibid, p.82.

24. Ibid, p.84

25. Ibid, p.86

26. Daily, Jaye (1977), "Non-print Material and Sound Recordings, Motion Pictures", in Marcel Dekker (Ed.) *Encyclopedia of Library and Information Science*, New York, Vol.20, p113.

27. Evans, G. Edward (2004), Ibid, p.91.

28. Katz, William A. (1980), *Collection Development: The Selection of Materials for Libraries*, Holt ,New York.

29. McGril, Rose Mary and Hickery Doryalyn (1984), *Acquisition Management and Collection Development*, ALA, Chicago.

30. Nazir Ahmad (1984), *Academic Libraries in Developing Society*, Qadiria, Lahore.

31. Drury, F.K.W(1930), *Book Selection.*

32. Mc Colvin, L.R (1925), *Theory of Book Selection for Public Libraries.*

33. Malvil Dewey quoted for Prasher, R.G. (1993), Op.cit, pp.64-65.

34. Ranganathan, S.R. (1988), *Library Manual*, 2nd ed., Sarada Ranganathan Endowment, Banglore, pp.185-186.

35. Schammel, Aliran, Ed. (2001), *Handbook of Information Management*, Aslib-umi, London.

36. Drury, F.K.W(1930), Op.cit.

37. Hicks, Warren B and Alma M Tillin (1970), *Developing Multimedia Libraries*, RR Bowker, New York, pp.16-18.

38. Scammell, Alison, Ed. (2001), Ibid. pp. 245-246.

39. Scammell, Alison, Ed. (2001), Ibid, pp.251-252.

40. Gelfand, M. A. (1974), *University Libraries for Developing Countries*, The University Book and Stationery, Delhi.

41. Evans, G. Edward (2004), Op.cit, p.315.

42. Katz, William A. (1980), Op.cit.

43. Cutter, Charles Ami (1904), *Rules of a Dictionary Catalogue*, 4th ed., GPO, Washington, p. 12.

44. Trevens, W. Stanley (1887), *The Principles of Science*, Macmillan, London, p. 12.

45. Shera, Jessee H (1966), *Libraries and Organization of Knowledge*, Crosby, London, p. 99.

46. Srivastava, Shyam Nath and Verma, Subash Chandra (1980), *University Libraries in India: Their Organization and Administration*, Sterling, New Delhi, p. 198.

47. The ALA Glossary of Library and Information Science (1983), ALA, Chicago.

48. Geer, Helen Thoranton (1955), *Charging Systems*, ALA, Chicago, p. 4.

49. Ranganathan, S. R. (1961), *Reference Service*, 2nd ed., Asia Publication, Bombay, p. 68

50. Ibid.

51. Rothstein, S. (1961), "Reference Service: New Dimensions in Librarianship", *College and Research Libraries*, Vol. 22, pp. 11-18.

52. Hutchins, Margaret (1944), *Introduction to Reference Work*, American Library Association, Chicago, p. 10.

53. Ranganathan, S. R. (1961), Op.cit., p. 27.

54. Krishna Kumar (1996), *Reference Service*, 5th rev. ed., Vikas Publication, New Delhi, p. 20.

55. Pal, S. S. (2004), *Special Library System and Information Services*, Icon Pub., New Delhi, p. 132

56. Esdaile A. (1969), *Esdaile's, Manual of Bibliography*, Allen and Unwin, London.

57. Pal, S. S. (2004), Op.cit., p. 136.

58. Ashworth, Wilfred (1979), *Special Libraries*, Clive Bingley, London, p. 121.

59. Prasher, R. G. (2003), *Information and its Communication*, Medallion, Ludhiana, p. 92.

60. British Standards Institution (1964), *Recommendations for the Preparation of Indexes For Books Periodicals and Other Publications*, London, (B. S. 3700: 1964), p. 6.

61. Pal, S. S. (2004), "Op.cit., p. 145

62. Vichery, B. C. (1965), *On Retrieval System Theory*, Buterworths, London, p. 154

63. Harrod's Librarians Glossary (1984), 5th ed. Grower pub. USA.

64. Luhn, H. P. (1961), "Selective Dissemination of New Scientific Information with the Aid of Electronic Processing Equipment", *American Documentation*, Vol. 12 No. 4, pp. 131-138.

65. Prasher, R. G. (2003), Op.cit., p. 172.

66. Bose, H. (1972), "Reprography in Documentation", in Goyal, S. P. (Ed.), *Indian Librarianship*, Scientific Books Store, Delhi, p. 29.

67. Hawkens, William R. (1966), *Copying Methods Manual*, ALA, Chicago, p. 356

68. Pal. S. S. (2004), Op.cit., p. 152.

69. Khan, M. T. M. (1997), *Information Organization and Communication*, Ess Ess Publication, New Delhi, p. 258.

70. Sharma, Jagdish Saran and Grover, D. R., (2004), "Reference Service and Sources of Information", New Delhi, Ess Ess Publication, p. 273

3

Librarians and Collection Development

The responsibility of collection development, its organization and services fall under the domain of librarian and acquisition librarian. The annals of history of library globally bears testimony to the fact that the librarian and acquisition librarians and at times even the library in-charge principally the teachers in-charge of library services have an enormous effect on shaping of library collections and their organization. Even in an era of globalization and age of knowledge management where the entire world has become one village as information available anywhere in the globe is available at the click of the mouse. It is hence that the role of librarians, acquisition librarians, collection development in charge remains ever-significant.

Against this background the author has surveyed the existing central university libraries of Uttar Pradesh to gauge the role of librarians and acquisition librarians as regards to the collection development, its organization and services.

METHODOLOGY

For the purpose of data collection from these libraries,

three (3) sets of questionnaires were designed, two (2) were for librarians, one main was for collecting information regarding collection development, organization and services and the other one was on information technology application. An additional questionnaire was prepared for the collection development in charge (mainly acquisition librarian) for gathering information pertaining to the organizational pattern of collection development.

The questionnaires were tested through conducting pilot study at Maulana Azad Library, AMU, Aligarh. The important suggestions made by the librarian and the acquisition in charge were incorporated while finalizing the questionnaire. The questionnaire was sent to the central university libraries of U.P. by mail. After short span of time, reminders were also sent but were unfortunately the requests were not entertained. Then the author personally visited the referred university libraries in order to ensure prompt returns and this in return created a chance for personal contact and observations. The author also got the opportunity of having personal interviews with librarians and acquisition in charge and thus got the questionnaire duly filled up. The survey per se was designed to be simple and very easy to answer, given the complexity of topic. Several "Yes/No" and single-word responses were included; with additional opportunity was provided for further comments on any given question, and fuller explanation was welcomed.

ANALYSIS AND DISCUSSION

Table 1. Library In-charge Profile and Library Timings

Profile and Timings	*AMU*	*BHU*	*ALU*	*BBAU*
Nature of Post of Librarian	Librarian-in-Charge	Prof. In-charge	Deputy Librarian	Librarian
Normal working days	18 hrs	11hrs	12hrs	07 hrs.
Sundays/Holidays	18	7	00	00
During Examinations	20	12	12	-
During vacations	18	11	12	-

Source: Questionnaire A, Question Nos. 1 & 2

At the very outset the author has further proceeded with the fact of knowing the library profile of the Central University Libraries (Henceforth AMU, BHU, ALU and BBAU).

As far as the nature of the post of librarian is concerned, AMU Library has an acting librarian for nearly six years. In fact, after the demise of full fledged librarian Prof. Noorul Hasan, no selection committee took place, owing to which acting librarian is carrying out the job of the Librarian. More recently a Selection Committee was held again and unfortunately no one was selected. A Professor from the Department of Library and Information Science (DLIS) is now looking often the library as Librarian-in-Charge, as a temporary measure. Whereas in BHU the work of the librarian is being executed by a Prof. in-Charge. Allahabad University (ALU) and BBAU are the two newly centralized universities which have full-fledged librarians.

Timing for accessing the library is different for these university libraries .It is revealed that AMU library functioning is considerably higher in all working days, including Sundays, Holidays, Examination and Vacations as compared to other three University Libraries under the study. The BHU, ALU and BBAU appear to have no specific time policy frame during the period of examinations and vacations. In case of AMU, it is manifested that during examination period and vacation the time slot have even increased taking into consideration the users' accessibility and their needs during these periods.

The table furnishes information regarding the qualifications and vacancy positions of the post of the main functionaries of the libraries under reference, such as, librarians, Deputy Librarians, Assistant Librarians, Documentation Officers, Information Scientists, Professional Assistants, Semi-Professional Assistants, Technical, and Clericals. The comparison of these libraries unfolds that AMU and BHU has larger chunk of supporting staff followed by ALU. The BBAU has one (1) Librarian only with three (3) supporting staff i.e. Professional Assistant, Semi-Professional Assistant and one unskilled staff. So far as BRAU is

Table 2. Number of Staff

Number of Staff	*AMU No of Posts*	*BHU No of Posts*	*BBAU No of Posts*	*ALU No of Posts*
Librarian	1	1	1	1
Deputy Librarian	5	3	-	1
Assist. Librarian	18	14	-	-
Documentation Officer	-	-	-	-
Information Scientist	-	1	-	-
Professional Assistant	16	14	1	-
Semi- Professional Assistant	38	37	1	-
Technical	18	1	-	5
Clerical	6	5	-	24
Supporting(unskilled)	22	48	1	33
Grand total	**114**	**124**	**4**	**64**

Source: Questionnaire A, Question No. 3

concerned, it is found that it is still at takeoff stage and therefore it will take some more time to build up requisite library staff.

Table 3. Approximate Size of the Library Printed Collection

Print Documents	*AMU*	*BHU*	*ALU*	*BBRAU*
Books/Monographs	1031528	1019717	606548	5421
Current journals (titles)	1029	825	450	42
Bound volumes of journals	-	100000	-	-
Research/Technical reports	-	-	-	-
Reference documents	-	-	-	-
Theses/ Dissertations	9492	9542	14057	-
Manuscripts	14575	7002	-	-
Seminar/Conference papers	-	-	-	-
Maps/charts/diagrams	3272	-	-	-
Patents/standards/ specifications	17813	-	-	-
Others	3507	-	-	-

Source: Questionnaire A, Question No. 4.1

The table reveals requisite information about the size of library collection in the form of print and electronic documents of the referred libraries of UP. It is discernible that print and electronic documents in AMU and BHU are sizeable as compared to ALU and BBAU. As a matter of fact AMU and BHU are the flagship universities among the Indian universities with more liberal and adequate funding than the newly centralized universities of ALU and BRAU. However, it is further discernible that ALU has larger number of books, periodicals etc. than BBAU. The author is of the opinion that this may be because of fact that ALU has been the oldest and star university of UP before assuming the status of a central university status. It is therefore presumed that the sizeable collection of documents has been obtained in legacy in the process of conversion from state university to Central University. This particular opinion of the author is further substantiated with the fact that the total numbers of theses, dissertations have also been completed in larger number in ALU i.e., numbering (14057). The AMU and BHU libraries are having these referred documents to the time of 9492 and 9542 which are less as compared to ALU. BHU has however remarkable feature of developing a rich collection of bound volumes of journals numbering almost one lac. This has not been done by any other university libraries under reference. So far as the other print documents are concerned especially current journals and manuscripts, AMU and BHU are found to be collecting sizeable number because of they being older libraries.. The AMU library is also found to be single unique library by having collections of maps, charts, diagrams, patents, standards, specification and rotographs etc.

As far as the development of collection of E-documents is concerned AMU occupies top slot, followed by BHU. The other two newly centralized university libraries under reference have almost negligible collection of e-documents except of course ALU having access to online internet databases numbering 75 and few CD-ROM databases. BHU distinguishes itself from AMU in terms of collection development of online journals to the tune of mammoth six

Table 4. Approximate Size of Electronic Documents

Electronic Documents	*AMU*	*BHU*	*ALU*	*BBAU*
CD-ROMs/ DVDs	2612	420	25	-
Online/Internet Databases	-	10	75	-
Online Journals	5000	6000	-	-
Video/Audio cassettes	1055	-	-	-
Microforms	1479	300	-	-
Others	304	-	-	-

Source: Questionnaire A, Question No. 4.1

thousand (6000) as compared to AMU with 5000. The CD-ROM, DVD, Floppies, microforms are found to have been satisfactorily collected and developed by AMU as compared to other university libraries under review: The author is of the view that with the intense revolution of IT in tandem with globalization of education, the AMU and the BHU are earnestly making sincere efforts to collect and develop both the print as well as the electronic documents in sync with the users' need to withstand the challenges pose by globalization and knowledge revolution .

Table 5. Current Primary and Secondary Journals of the Libraries

Current primary and secondary journals	*AMU*				*BHU*				*ALU*				*BBAU*			
	Pri.		*Sec.*		*Pri.*		*Sec.*		*Pri.*		*Sec.*		*Pri.*		*Sec.*	
	P.	*O.*	*P.*	*O.*	*P.*	*O.*	*P.*	*O.*	*P.*	*O.*	*P.*	*O.*	*P.*	*O.*	*P.*	*O.*
Indian	587	—	06	—	491	—	07		298		03					—
Foreign	420	—	16	—	323	—	04		141		08					—

Source: Questionnaire – A, Question No. 4.2

The analysis of the total break up of the current primary and secondary journals reveals that three university libraries of AMU, BHU and ALU have collected and developed primary and secondary Indian and foreign journals both. The BBAU, being a new central university, either has no such provision.

Table 6. Participation in Consortia by the Libraries

Participate in any of the following Library Consortia	*AMU*	*BHU*	*ALU*	*BBAU*	*Total Population 100%*
UGC-INFONET	Y	Y	Y	N	75
INDEST	N	N	N	N	0
ICMR E-journal Consortia	N	N	N	N	0
CSIR E-journal Consortia	N	N	N	N	0
Others	N	N	N	N	0

Source: Questionnaire – A, Question No. 4.3

With the advent of present day information era, participation in library consortia became necessary in order to get information globally for library information professionals. When questioned of their participation in any of the library consortia, the librarians have emphatically replied in negative in case of participation through INDEST, ICMR, and others including International e-journals Consortia. However it has been learnt that recently AMU Library has started participating in INDEST. However, other three universities are found to have been participated in UGC Infonet Consortia'. From the author's perspective, the cardinal reason for not partaking at the echelon of national and international consortia may be attributed to paucity of funds and lack of definite collection development policy relating to electronic resources. The author further observes that lack of professionalization in terms of current knowledge pertaining to collection development, its organization and services may be yet another reason. To keep pace with rapid changes in the sphere of collection development domain, librarians, acquisition in charge and other supporting staff need to undergo training and refresher's programme from time to time. Library development centric programmes would be instrumental and they shall equip the libraries with the contemporary and latest collection development policies, schemes and programmes, researches and innovative collection development, its organization and services products.

Table 7. Comparative Growth of Books and Periodicals in the Libraries during (1985-86 to 2005-06)

Print Documents	*1985-86*	*1990-91*	*1995-96*	*2000-01*	*2005-06*	*% Growth*
Books/Monographs						
AMU	680597	789362.0	884703	965069.0	1071524	57.4
BHU	711603	783117	854116	916821	977669	37.39
ALU	311246	432345	521344	572111	601523	93.26
BBAU	——	—	——	3428	5421	58.13
Journals /periodical/magz.						
AMU	2075	1325	1382	1073	1029	-50.40
BHU	2049	2075	1844	1355	910	-55.58
ALU	743	851	922	1121	1072	44.27
BBAU	——	——	—	28	42	50

Source: Questionnaire, Question No. 4.4

This comparative table has been made in order to determine and show the growth in-print documents of all the university libraries for the period from 1985-86 to 2005-06. It is discernible from the table that the number of books and monographs collection by AMU was 680597 in 1985-86 which increased to 1071524 in 2005-06 registering an annual average growth of 57%. The BHU has developed collection of books and monographs from 711603 to 977669 in the same period with an annual growth rate 37.4%. ALU developed the collection of books and monographs to the order of 311246 in 1985-86 which increased to 601523 in 2005-06 showing an annual growth rate of 93%. BBAU, the newly centralized university, developed collection books and monographs numbering 3428 in 2000-01 which increased to 5421 in 2005-06 registering a growth rate of 58%. The overall comparison manifests the fact that in spite of the newly centralized university libraries ALU and BBAU having smaller chunk of books and monographs as compared to AMU and BHU yet the annual average growth rate calculated is higher during this period.

In case of the development of collection of Journals/ periodicals/maps the negative growth trends are discernible in the case of AMU and BHU. The reasons may be ascribed to the fact that with the IT boom in the country in consonance with globalization of education the world over, these two traditional centralized universities while acknowledging the users needs, imbibed the method of developing the collection of journals/periodicals through on-line subscription and also kicked off brisk participation in consortia. The new centralized universities have also set up the collection of journals/periodicals/maps during this period. The author feels that since these university libraries are not much IT and IT savvy, so they are also found to be inadequately subscribing to the requisite on-line journals and periodicals.

Table 8. Comparative Growth of Libraries Budget from 1985-86 to 2005-06

LIBRARY BUDGET	*AMU*	*BHU*	*ALU*	*BBAU*
1985-86	5408540	-	440000	-
1990-91	10212210	10000000	800000	-
1995-96	14542700	17500000	1150000	-
2000-01	27647000	19700000	1600000	1232000
2005-06	43301000	30000000	9154600	2505000
Overall Growth	700.60%	200%	1980.59%	103%

Source: Questionnaire A, question No. 5.1

The comparative growth of the budget of central university libraries has also been studied by the author during the period from 1985-86 to 2005-06.

It is indicative that ALU is ahead in terms of growth of library budget of all the reviewed universities. The second slot is occupied by AMU, followed by BHU and BBAU. The main cause of ALU occupying top slot is that special grant was given at the time of assuming central university status to it.

Table 9. Provision of Separate Budget for Online Journal/Database

Provision of Separate Budget for Online Journals/ Database	*AMU*	*BHU*	*ALU*	*BBAU*	*Total Population 100%*
Yes	—	—	—	—	0
No	N	N	N	N	100
Cant Say					

Source : Questionnaire A, Question No. 5.2 (a)

The librarians of these universities were served a question with regard to separate budget for on-line journals and databases. It is quite dismaying to note that none of the librarians have answered in affirmative. The rational for making no provision for separate budget for on-line journal and databases may be either owing to the paucity of funds or deficit of clear-cut authority to dispense with funds for the purpose. Further, it is observed that the purported funds are rationed to different departments. The Heads of the departments and the librarian are the users of these funds

Table 10. Alternative Method to Acquire Online Journals and Databases

Alternative method to acquire online Journals and Databases	*AMU*	*BHU*	*ALU*	*BBAU*	*Total Population 100%*	
					Yes	*No*
No						
Through UGC-Infonet Consortia	Y	Y	Y	N	75	25
Canceling some print subscription	Y	Y	Y	N	75	25
Acquiring only those which are available	Y	N	N	N	25	75
Acquiring only those which are freely	Y	N	N	N	25	75

Source: Questionnaire – A, Question No. 5 2(b)

as per the budget allocation by the finance department. However, the Heads of the departments and librarians are supposed to submit annual budget plans and schemes and make their own priority policy frame. It seems that in these libraries, no separate budget for on-line journals/databases have been put forward.

However, on asking a question by the author with regard to alternative methods to acquire online journals and databases, librarians of these universities offered divergent answers. It is detectable that 75% of the respondents endorsed that they procure on-line journals/databases through UGC-Infonet consortia. However, BBAU negated the use of this method for acquiring on-line journals and databases. In fact, 75% of the total respondents i.e., librarians of AMU, BHU and ALU expressed that they adopt alternative methods to acquiring on-line journals and databases by canceling some print subscriptions. In case of the questions with regard to acquisition and free on-line databases, 75% of the respondents i.e. BHU, ALU, BBAU declined adopting this method whereas 25% respondents i.e. the librarian of AMU expressed that he adopts alternative method to acquire on-line journals/databases based on their availability without cost.

Table 11. Adequacy of Library Budget

Adequacy of	*AMU*		*BHU*		*ALU*		*BBAU*		*Total Population 100%*	
library budget for	*Yes*	*No*	*Yes*	*No*	*Yes*	*No*	*Yes*	*No*	*Yes*	*No*
Print Journals	—	N	—	N	—	N	—	N	0	100
Online Journals	—	N	—	N	—	N	—	N	0	100

Source: Questionnaire A, Question No. 5.3

The author asked a question to find out the adequacy of budget for print journals as well as on-line journals. It is manifested from the survey that the budget for subscription to print and on-line journals is quite inadequate.

Table 12. Assessment of Users Need

Assessment of user's needs	*AMU*	*BHU*	*ALU*	*BBAU*	*Total Population100%*
Yes	Y	Y	Y	N	75
No	—	—	—	—	00
Cant Say					

Source: Questionnaire – A, Question No. 6.1

Table 13. Methods Adopted for Assessment of User's Need

Methods adopted for assessment of user's need	*AMU*	*BHU*	*ALU*	*BBAU*	*Total population 100%*	
					Yes	*No*
Yes						
Studies on collection use	Y	Y	Y	N	75	25
User's surveys	N	N	N	N	0	100
Any other	Requisition from departments and students	N	N	N	25	75

Source: Questionnaire – A, Question No. 6.2

The author has further asked few more questions to know from the librarian of universities as regards the assessment of user's needs and methods adopted for assessment their needs (Tables 12 & 13). All librarians confirmed that they do consider and assess the users need from time to time. Except, the librarian of BBAU negated about this kind of assessment. The librarians also confirmed the fact that they assess the users' need, based on the use of collection. However, on the contrary all the respondents under survey declined to adopt any method based on users' survey to assess the users need. The AMU librarian confirmed that the method of assessing users need is also based on the requisition from the respective departments and the students. It is, however, observed from the survey as regards assessment of user's need that there does not exist a clear clear policy of assessing the user's needs in libraries.

Table 14. Response of Libraries about Collection Development Policy

Collection Development Policy	*AMU*	*BHU*	*ALU*	*BBAU*	*Total Population 100%*
Yes	Y	—	Y	—	50
No	—	N	—	N	50
Cant Say					

Source: Questionnaire – A, Question No. 7.1

Table 15. Authority of Library Involved in Creating and Approving Collection Development Policy

Authority responsible for creating and approving collection development policies	*AMU*	*BHU*	*ALU*	*BBAU*
Director	—	—	—	—
Librarian	Y	—	—	—
Library Committee	—	—	Y	—
Collection Development Committee	—	—	—	—
Acquisition Librarian	Y	—	—	—
Other	Purchase Committee	—	—	—

Source: Questionnaire – A, Question No. 7.2

Table 16. Response about Revision of Collection Development Policy

Revision of collection development policy	*AMU*	*BHU*	*ALU*	*BBAU*	*Total Population 100%*
Yes	Y	—	—	—	25
No	—	N	N	N	75
Cant Say					

Source: Questionnaire – A, Question No. 7.3

There were also questions designed to know from the librarians related to collection development policy, the extent of authority of the librarian involved in creating a collection development policy and revising it if they have one .(Tables 14, 15 & 16). Out of the total respondents under survey, 50% accepted that there is collection development policy whereas the other 50% respondents from BHU and BBAU reiterated that there is no such collection development policy. The authority for creating and approving collection development policy in case of AMU lies with the librarian and acquisition in charge whereas in case of ALU the authority lies with the library committee. In case of AMU, for bulk purchase there is a purchase committee. The librarians of BHU and BBAU have not been asked the question of authority, on the first instance as they declined existence of any collection development policy. Similarly, on the question of the revision of collection development policy only librarian of AMU disclosed the fact of existence of revision of collection development policy whereas librarians of BHU, ALU, and BBAU responded that there does not exist the revision of collection development policy. As regards the time frame for revision of collection development policy, none of the librarians under reference responded to this question. The author perceives that their unwillingness to answer this question may be owing to the non-existence of specific revision policy about collection development.

Table 17. Separate Policy for E-documents

Separate policy document(s) for E-Documents?	*AMU*	*BHU*	*ALU*	*BBAU*	*Total Population 100%*
Yes	Y	NR-	NR	NR	25
No	NR	NR-	NR	NR	00
Cant Say					

Source: Questionnaire – A, Question No. 7.4

In congruence with this question, another question was designed for the librarians pertaining to on collection development policy for E-documents. Out of the total respondents, the librarian from AMU confirmed that there is a separate policy for E-documents including the electronic resources such as CD/DVD-ROMs, and fee based or subscription resource/databases available via Internet and freely available (non-free, non-subscriptions resource/ database available via Internet).

Table 18. Plan to formulate a Collection Development Policy of Libraries in Future

Plan to formulate a collection development policy IN FUTURE	*AMU*	*BHU*	*ALU*	*BBAU*	*Total Population 100%*
Yes	Y	Y	Y	Y	100
No	—	—	—	—	—
Cant Say					

Source: Questionnaire – A, question No. 7.5

In order to appreciate the future plan of a collection development policy of libraries, the responses of respondents were analyzed. It has been petered out from the responses that all the librarians under review felt the urgency of carving a future strategy or policy with regard to collection development policy. (Table 18)

Table 19. Method Used by Librarian to Identify Documents for Selection

Usually identify documents for selection	*AMU*	*BHU*	*ALU*	*BBAU*	*Total Population 100%*
Searching publisher's web sites	Y	Y	Y	—	75
Subject Bibliography	-	Y	Y	Y	75
Check the holdings of other libraries	—	—	—	Y	25

Indian National Bibliography	—	Y	Y	Y	75
Faculty and users recommendations	Y	Y	Y	Y	100
Guide to Indian periodical literature	Y	—	Y	—	50
Ulrich International periodical Directory	Y	Y	Y	Y	100
Directory of Internet/ online databases	—	—	Y	—	25
Publisher's Catalogue	Y	Y	Y	Y	100
Cumulative Book Index	—	—	—	—	
Other		—	—		

Source: Questionnaire – A, Question No. 8.1

The author has also asked a question to know the methods applied for selection of documents.

It is evident from the table 19 that 75% respondents answered that their selection for documents is generally based on searching publisher's websites. The librarian of BBAU did not confirm such kind of method to identify documents for selection. BHU, ALU, and BBAU constituting 75% of the total respondents indicated that they adopt subject bibliography method for document selection. The librarian of BBAU which constitutes 25% of the total respondents said the selection is based on the checking of the holding of other libraries. The librarians of BHU, ALU, and BBRAU said that the basis for document selection is mainly done through scanning sources such as Indian National Bibliography. On the paratemeters of identifying documents for selection based on the recommendations of Faculty and Users the total respondents answered in affirmative. The librarians of AMU and ALU confirmed that they identify documents for selection though Indian periodical literature. On the other hand the total respondents of all the four librarians said that they go for selecting documents by largely identifying documents based on International periodical Directories. The librarian of ALU disclosed an unique method for the identification of document selection based on directory of Internet/online database. The remaining three librarians did not confirm that they go for this method. The method of selection based on published catalogue seems very popular as all the librarians confirmed this fact.

Table 20. Authorities Responsible for Selecting Documents

Authority / Authorities responsible for selecting documents.	*AMU*	*BHU*	*ALU*	*BBAU*	*Total Population 100%*
Library committee	—	—	Y	—	25
Book selection committee	—	Y	—	—	25
Head of the institute	Y	Y	—	Y	75
Librarian	Y	Y	Y	Y	100
Concerned faculty	Y	Y	Y	Y	100
OTHER	Head acquisition division	—	—	—	25

Source: Questionnaire – A, Question No. 8.2

The question on the authority responsible for selecting the document was also put forth to the librarians (Table 20). It is found out that Head of the Institute, Librarian and the Head of the concerned faculty are the people responsible for selecting the documents in almost all the libraries under reference. On the other hand at BHU and ALU, the librarians have averred that their library committees and book selection committees are also responsible for selection. In case of AMU the librarian has confirmed that sometimes the responsibility for the selection of documents lies with the Head of Acquisition division.

Any method for selecting and evaluating the quality and relevance of the documents are centered on certain norms and yardsticks. In this regard, the author has designed few questions for the librarians and tried to survey such as quality review and users' needs in relation to subject relevance.

Table 21. Criteria Followed by Librarian to Evaluate the Documents

Criteria Followed to Evaluate the Documents	*AMU*	*BHU*	*ALU*	*BBAU*	*Total Population 100%*
Quality (based on review, user needs, etc.)	Y	—	Y	Y	75
Subject relevance	Y	Y	Y	Y	100
Currency, Authority, Completeness	Y	Y	Y	—	75
Language	—	Y	Y	—	50
Uniqueness of contents	Y	Y	Y	—	75
Relevance of materials for curriculum	Y	Y	Y	Y	100
Relevance of materials for faculty/research	Y	Y	Y	Y	100
Cost effectiveness	Y	Y	Y	Y	100
Trial before use	—	—	—	—	
Network compatibility	—	—	—	—	
Hardware/Software compatibility	—	—	Y	—	25
Strength of search engine/access points	—	—	—	—	
Remote accessibility	—	—	—	—	
OTHER	—	—	—	—	

Source: Questionnaire – A, Question No. 8.3

It is obvious from Table-21 that the greater number of respondents (ranging from 75% to 100%)use subject relevance, users' need, currency, authority, completeness, uniquesses of contents, relevance of matter, economical to evaluate the qualitativeness of the documents.

The network compatibility, hardware and software strength of search engines and access points and remote accessibility are the quality parameters from the view point of IT and IT Enabled Services in an era of globalized knowledge economy. The ALU librarian is the only one considering hardware and software compatibility to evaluate the quality aspects of the documents. The indicators should also bring in computing components for composite criteria to be adhered to by the librarians to assess the quality documents.

Table 22. Methods Used for Acquisition of Documents

Method(s) used for acquisition of documents	*AMU*	*BHU*	*ALU*	*BBAU*	*Total Population 100%*
Approval system	Y	Y	Y	Y	100
Confirmed order system	Y	Y	Y	Y	100
Not fixed system	—	—	—	—	
Other (please specify)		—	—	—	—

Source: Questionnaire – A, Question No. 8.4

On this question in relation to adopting methods used for acquisition of documents in the overall policy of collection development and acquisition the respondents have confirmed two methods, viz. approval system, and confirmed order system.

Table 23. Channels for Acquiring Documents

Channel(s) for acquiring documents	*AMU*	*BHU*	*ALU*	*BBAU*	*Total Population 100%*
Online database vendors	—	—	—	—	
Publishers	Y	Y	Y	Y	100
Distributors	Y	Y	Y	Y	100
Gift/Exchange	Y	Y	Y	Y	100
Free downloads from Internet/WWW	Y	—	Y	—	50
Other (please specify)	—	—	—	—	—

Source: Questionnaire – A, Question No. 8.5

In conformity with this question, another question was asked relating to the channels for acquiring documents (Table 23). All respondents have confirmed that they acquire documents through publishers, distributors and by gifts and exchange. AMU and ALU revealed that they also acquire documents through free downloads from Internet and www. The channels for acquiring documents from on-line database vendors have not been indicated at all.

The author has found that it is owing to the soaring cost associated with this method has kept the librarians away from adopting this particular channel.

Table 24. Problems Faced by Libraries in the Acquiring of Documents

Problem Faced by Libraries in the Acquiring Documents	*AMU*	*BHU*	*ALU*	*BBAU*	*Total Population 100%*
Lack of funds	Y	—	—	Y	50
Lack of infrastructure to support storage and access	—	—	—	Y	25
Lack of expertise for management	—	—	—	Y	25
Lack of autonomy	—	—	—	Y	25
Other (please specify)	—	—	—	—	—

Source: Questionnaire – A, Question No. 8.6(b)

Table 25. Participation in Resource Sharing

Participate in resource Sharing	*AMU*	*BHU*	*ALU*	*BBRAU*	*Total Population 100%*
Yes	—	—	—	—	
No	N	N	N	N	100
Cant Say					

Source: Questionnaire – A, Question No. 9.1

The librarians have not cited any specific problem in acquiring documents. However, the paucity of funds, unsatisfactory infrastructure is the undistinguished grey areas being encountered by newly centralized university. (Table 24). While inquiring regarding the level of participation in resource sharing, all the respondents have negated out such kind of efforts. (Table - 25)

Table 26. Weeding out of Documents

Weeding out of Documents	*AMU*	*BHU*	*ALU*	*BBAU*	*Total Population 100%*
Rules	—	—	—	—	
Obsolete material	Y	—	—	—	25
As per local Rules	—	—	—	—	

Source: Questionnaire – A, Question No. 10.2

Table 27. Time Span of Weeding out of Documents

Weeding out of Documents	*AMU*	*BHU*	*ALU*	*BBAU*	*Total Population 100%*
Annually	Y	—	—	—	25
After five years	—	—	—	—	
After Ten years	—	—	—	—	
On Adhoc basis.	Y	—	—	—	25

Source: Questionnaire – A, Question No. 10.3

The process of weeding out of documents in terms of their obsolescence has only been done by the AMU on the annual and adhoc basis as has been confirmed by the librarian of AMU. (Tables 26 & 27).

The assessment and evaluation of the collection based on certain criteria is yet another important question asked by author. It is quite significant to note from Table-28 that AMU and BHU for evaluating their collection use the criteria of total amount of funds spent, number of books added, number of books borrowed for study and number of books consulted in the library.

Table 28. Criteria used for Collection Evaluation

Criteria of collection evaluation?	*AMU*	*BHU*	*ALU*	*BBAU*	*Total Population 100%*
Amount of funds spent	Y	Y	N	N	50
No. of books added	Y	Y	——	—	50
No. of books ordered but not received	——	—	—	—	
No. of books borrowed for home study	Y	Y	—	—	50
No. of books consulted in the library	Y	Y	—	—	50
No. of books received on ILL from library	—	—	——	—	
Any other, please specify	——	—	——	—	

Source: Questionnaire – A, Question No. 11.2

Table 29. System Followed for Classifying the Documents

System Followed	*AMU*	*BHU*	*ALU*	*BBAU*	*Total Population 100%*
DDC with edition	Y 18th	——	Y 21st	Y 19th	75
UDC with edition	—	——	—	—	
CC with edition	——	Y 6th	——	—	25
Modified with edition	——	——	——	—	

Source : Questionnaire – A, Question No. 12.1

A question has been shaped for the respondents to be cognizant of the system followed for classification and cataloguing of the documents. (Table-29 & 30). It is discernible from the table that out of the four commonly used system, such as, DDC, CC, UDC and modified, librarians of AMU, ALU, and BBAU are found to have been following DDC system whereas the librarian of BHU confirmed following CC.

On the question of cataloging code used, AMU, BHU and ALU said that they use AACR-2 cataloging code.

Table 30. Cataloging Code Used in Libraries

Cataloguing Code Used	*AMU*	*BHU*	*ALU*	*BBRAU*	*Total Population 100%*
ALA	—	—	—	—	
AACR 2	Y	Y	Y	—	75
AACR 2	—	—	—	—	
CCC	—	—	—	—	
Modified	—	—	—	—	

Source : Questionnaire – A, Question No. 12.2

The author has also asked a question pertaining to the accesses to documents made by the libraries. It has been found out that AMU and BHU have both open access and closed access; whereas the university libraries of ALU and BBAU have only one system i.e., closed system. In AMU and BHU, the users are permitted to make use of the documents within library premises as well as outside the library.

Table 31. Availability of Professionals for Reference Desk

Full Time Professional for Reference Desk	*AMU*	*BHU*	*ALU*	*BBAU*	*Total Population 100%*
Yes	Y	Y	—	—	50
No	—	—	N	N	50
Cant Say	—	—	—	—	

Source: Questionnaire – A, Question No. 13.1

On the question of availability of professionals for reference desk (Table 31) it is revealed that only librarians of AMU and BHU gave answer in affirmative showing that they have full time professionals for reference desk. On the other hand librarians of ALU and BBAU gave negative responses symbolizing that there is no such provision for appointing full time professionals for reference desk.

Table 32. Approaches of Professional to Reader during Querry

When a reader approaches you with a query, do you	*AMU*		*BHU*		*ALU*		*BBAU*		*Total Population 100%*	
	Yes	*No*	*Yes*	*No*	*Yes*	*No*	*Yes*	*No*	*Yes*	*No*
Direct him to the catalogue/ OPAC?	Y	—	Y	—	Y	—	Y	—	100	0
Direct him to the shelf?	—	N	Y	—	Y	—	—	N	50	50
Bring the reference source and give him?	Y	—	Y	—	—	N	—	N	50	50
Show him the page where information exists?	Y	—	—	N	—	N	—	N	25	75
Give him information itself?	Y	—	Y	—	Y	—	—	N	75	25
Direct him to the Electronic Sources?	—	N	Y	—	Y	—	—	N	50	50

Source: Questionnaire – A, Question No. 13.2

The author has also put forth questions regarding readers' approach with a query related to reference materials. It is manifest from Table-32 that all the librarians direct the readers to the catalogue/OPAC.

On the question of the availability of reprographic facilities the respondents except BBAU have confirmed that this particular facility is available to staff, faculty members, research scholars, students as well as outsiders.

Table 33. Reprographic Service

Facility available to	*AMU*	*BHU*	*ALU*	*BBAU*	*Total Population 100%*
Staff	Y	Y	Y	N	75
Faculty members	Y	Y	Y	N	75
Research scholars	Y	Y	Y	N	75
Students	Y	Y	Y	N	75
Outsiders	Y	Y	Y	N	75

Source: Questionnaire – A, Question No. 14

Table 34. Provision of Classified Services

Services	*No. of Response Old Centralized University*		*No. of Response Newly Centralized University*		*Total 100%*
	AMU	*BHU*	*ALU*	*BBRAU*	
	Yes NR NQ	*Yes NR NQ*	*Yes NR NQ*	*Yes NR NQ*	
Microfilim Service	Y	N	N	N	25%
Information Service	Y	Y	Y	N	75%
Inter Library Loan Facility	N	N	N	N	0%
Translation Service	N	N	N	N	0%
CAS	Y	Y	Y	N	75%
SDI	N	N	N	N	0%
Bibliography	Y	Y	Y	N	75%
CD/DVD ROM	N	Y	Y	N	50%
Online Service	Y	Y	Y	N	75%
Online Journals/ Database	Y	Y	Y	N	75%

Source: Questionnaire – A, Question No. 15

On the question of the availability of microfilm services the librarian of AMU has confirmed this service whereas the librarians of BHU, ALU and BBRAU revealed that they have no provision of this service (Table-34). As far as other important services, such as, Information services,

Bibliography, CAS, on-line service, on-line journals and database are concerned, the librarians of AMU, BHU and ALU acknowledged that they facilitate for these services to the user. On the contrary, the BBAU informed the non-availability of such service in the library. In modern IT era, CD and DVD version of bulky information is considered a handy for the users of library. It has been disclosed that only BHU and ALU libraries provide CD and DVD- ROM service, which shows that only 50% of total population are able to exploit the IT-centric gadgets.

On the question of sending information to faculty and other users pertaining to the materials received regarding their fields of interests answered that they do inform the users including the faculty of the university. However, the librarians have divergent views with regard to maintaining readers' profile. The AMU and BBAU librarians have replied that they do not maintain readers profile whereas the other two libraries i.e., ALU and BHU confirm that they do maintain the reader's interest profile.

Table 35. Information Services

Information Services	*AMU*		*BHU*		*ALU*		*BBAU*		*Total Population 100%*	
	Yes	*No*	*Yes*	*No*	*Yes*	*No*	*Yes*	*No*	*Yes*	*No*
Send information about the materials received regarding their field of interest to the faculty?	Y	—	Y	—	Y	—	Y	—	100	0
Maintained a reader's interest profile	—	N	Y	—	Y	—	—	N	50	50
Readers come to see the books/ journals on receiving the information?	Y	—	Y	—	Y	—	—	N	75	25

Source : Questionnaire – A. Question No. 16

The readers and the users of the information then are found to have come to see the books and journals upon receiving the information. 75% of the respondents confirmed that their users and faculty members do come to consult the books and journals after their arrival in their library. (Table-35).

Table 36. Periodical Section in Libraries

Periodical Services	*AMU*		*BHU*		*ALU*		*BBAU*		*Total Population 100%*	
	Yes	*No*	*Yes*	*No*	*Yes*	*No*	*Yes*	*No*	*Yes*	*No*
Separate Periodical section?	Y	—	Y	—	Y	—	—	N	75	25
You circulate loose issues of Periodicals	Y	—	Y	—	Y	—	Y	—	100	0

Source: Questionnaire – A, Question No. 17

Few questions were also designed by the author to the effect that whether the libraries maintain separate periodical section, and circulate loose issues of periodicals (Table 36). AMU, BHU and ALU confirmed that they have an exclusive separate periodical section while the librarian of BBAU did not confirm this kind of provision existing in the library. Upon the circulation of the loose issues of periodicals to the users every one replied that they circulate the loose issue periodicals to the users and faculty members of the universities under review.

On-line access is the most sought after services, which the libraries have started to provide. In this very line, the scholar put forth the question upon the availability of on-line access to documents, such as, on-line journals and databases, internet for global access to library users. The answers of respondents are found divergent. The librarians of AMU and ALU informed that they provide accessibility on intranet for users' within the library. The librarians of BHU and BBAU did not inform about this facility. On campus

Table 37. Availability of Online Access to the Documents

Access to online Journals/ Databases and Documents	*AMU*	*BHU*	*ALU*	*BBAU*	*Total Population 100%*
Yes					
On library Intranet, for users within the library	Y	—	Y	—	50
On campus Intranet, for Institute/ campus only	—	Y	Y	—	50
On Internet for library users only	—	—	Y	—	25
On Internet for global access	—	—	—	—	
No					
Lack of Online Journals/ Databases	—	—	—	Y	25
Lack of infrastructure to support access	—	—	—	Y	25

Source : Questionnaire – A, Question No. 18

intranet for institute and campus, the librarians of BHU and ALU confirmed this kind of service whereas the librarian of AMU and BBAU did not confirm this particular service being provided to the users. The service of Internet for library users

Table 38. Kind of User Education Training

Name of the Training Offers to User's	*AMU*	*BHU*	*ALU*	*BBAU*	*Total Population 100%*
Computer training	Y	Y	Y		75
Searching CD-ROM/ online databases	—	Y	Y	—	50
Searching online journals	Y	—	Y	—	50
Searching Internet/WWW	Y	—	Y	—	50
Other	—	—	—	—	

Source: Questionnaire – A, Question No. 19

was only confirmed by the librarian of Allahabad University, while BBAU reported that there are lack of on-line journals and databases service and there is no infrastructure to support access.

The author also devised questions pertaining to the facility of training and the kind of training being offered to library staff and the users (Table-38). So far as computer training is concerned, the libraries of AMU, BHU and ALU have answered in affirmative reiterating that they provide training to library staff such as getting access to internet, www, FTP etc., how to handle on-line journals and databases etc. However, this particular service of computer training is not offered by BBAU. The librarians of BHU and ALU informed that they have the service for searching CD-ROMs whereas the librarians of AMU and BBAU did not confirm to this service. The librarians of AMU and ALU have a service for searching on-line journals and internet, www, whereas remaining librarian of BHU and BBAU did not back up this kind of service.

CONCLUSION

It is cogently demonstrated from analysis that print and electronic document collection in AMU and BHU tends to be larger. The AMU and BHU as a matter of fact are the flagship universities among Indian Universities with more funding than the relatively newly centralized universities of ALU and BBAU. However, it is also discernible that ALU has larger number of books; periodicals etc. because of fact that ALU has been the oldest university of UP before assuming the central university status. The total collection of theses and dissertations has been completed in larger numbers in ALU than in AMU and BHU. It has been strongly perceived from the analysis that BHU has significant number of bound volumes of journals numbering around one lac. This feat has not been achieved by any central university library. Current journals are found to be in considerable number at AMU and BHU. More interestingly it has unfolded through the analysis that AMU library is found to be the only library, developing collection of special materials such as maps, charts, diagrams, patents, standards, specification and rotographs. It is also observed that as far as size of the collection of electronic documents are considered; AMU occupies the top echelon followed by BHU. Only ALU is having on-line internet databases numbering 75 and some CD-ROM databases as well.

AMU and BHU are making wholesome endeavors to garner and develop print and electronic documents in sync with the users need to sustain their intensity of challenge of knowledge revolution and globalization. A good number of current, primary and secondary Indian and foreign journals have been collected by AMU, BHU and ALU. They are also participating in UGC-Infonet consortia. All the libraries have no room for budget for on-line journals and databases. In fact AMU, BHU and ALU use different mode to procure on-line journals and databases through UGC-Infonet consortia. They also adopt alternative methods to acquire on-line journals and databases nullifying some print subscriptions. However, the budget for prints and on-line journals for all the libraries is inadequate.

The AMU, BHU and ALU assess the users' needs from time to time based on the use of their collection. AMU adopts the method of assessing users' needs based on requisition from departments and students. They in fact adopt the method of assessing users' nccds based on requisition from departments and students. All these libraries do not have clear cut policy as regards the assessment of users' need.

Authority of creating and approving collection development policy in the AMU lies with the librarian and acquisition librarian. In case of ALU, it lies with library committee. In case of AMU for bulk purchase there is a purchase committee. Only AMU disclosed the fact of the existence of revision of collection development policy and it has a separate collection development policy for E-documents as well. All the libraries under review, feel the need of appropriately putting in place a future strategy or policy with regard to collection development.

It is also observed that there is a cardinal authority responsible for selecting documents in almost all the libraries. AMU, BHU and ALU follow certain yardstick for selecting and evaluating quality documents, such as, subject relevance, users need, currency, authority, completeness, uniqueness of contents, cost effectiveness.

All these libraries have adopted both approval system followed by confirmed order system for acquisition of documents and they also acquire documents through publishers, distributors and gifts and exchanges. Weeding of documents in terms of obsolete of material has only been done by the AMU on an annual as well as adhoc basis. Mainly AMU and BHU adopt criteria for evaluation of their collection. AMU, BHU and ALU are providing reference services, information service, bibliography service, on-line service, CAS, On-line journals and databases to their users. BBAU has only book lending service. CD/DVD-ROM service is being provided by BHU and ALU. Only AMU is providing Microfilm service as well. Translation service, SDI, Inter library loan services are not being provided by any of these libraries. AMU, BHU, ALU have maintained separate periodical section and circulate loose issues of periodicals. AMU and ALU also have the facility to access on-line journals and databases through campus intranet for users with in the library. AMU, BHU and ALU have provided computer related training to staff and users too.

4

Organizational Pattern of Collection Development

Collection development has a legacy of being analogous to the organization of library services in university libraries. There are several umpteen studies which reveal the pace and development of collection. It is indeed an unshared domain of the librarian and the teaching faculty and rarely the university acquisition librarian. These individuals had a tremendous influence in fashioning of library collection during previous century. As the libraries became larger and more complex, as the budgets for materials grew, and also as the librarian's status within the academic community gained credibility, the responsibility for collection development began to rope in more people. The most common structure was that of the acquisition department still working closely with the help of the teaching faculty. As more and more libraries acknowledged the urgency to increase the number of professional staffs, many different organizational patterns were developed including collection development. However, the functions of collection development were never clearly defined as that of the other functions in the libraries.

Cataloging was always considered a technical service; reference was always considered a public service. The question most librarians had to encounter was as to where to place collection development in administrative scheme of things. In Indian libraries especially in university libraries, Acquisition departments naturally enveloped the responsibility of the collection development function.

The response to this survey was quite gratifying. The first five questions were devised to find out as to whom in the library the responsibility for collection development and the span of control had assigned. All of them denied that the librarians are not administratively in-charge of collection development in their respective libraries.

To spell out the administrative role for the collection development, each person surveyed was asked to specify their exact responsibility and to whom they reports and how each would classify their position. The designations varied. However, the titles indicated that the collection development person in-charge is placed at the level of assistant librarian, if not the librarian. In some cases the designation also indicated an additional responsibility. When asked specifically to classify their positions by level, librarians of AMU, BHU said that their positions were at the level of Assistant Librarians who are responsible for acquisition. The librarians of ALU and BBAU responded that their positions were classified as Chief Librarian. In ALU ad BBAU, no Assistant Librarian is available; therefore, chief librarian is the head of all collection development activities as well as other functions of the library. Primarily the librarians of ALU and BBAU specified no collection development unit in their library. The librarians of AMU and BHU consider collection development as an important function. In AMU and BHU collection development in charge :acquisition Librarian, report to university librarian and university librarian reports to Registrar whereas in ALU and BBAU University the librarians, who are also In charge of collection development report to the Registrar.

A more complex issue, i.e. the organizational structure of collection development within central university libraries, was to be determined by the next set of questions. AMU and BHU have placed it in acquisition section, while librarians of ALU and BBAU responded that there are no collection development units in their libraries.

The answer to the question about the span of control of collection development in-charge, all respondents indicated holding responsibility of acquisitions, preservation and gift and exchange. In a correlated question, the librarians were asked what additional functions were attached to the collection development unit, the librarians of AMU and BHU responded that they are responsible for acquisition function.

To determine the span of control that collection development librarian have over personnel, they were first asked how many people report to them directly. The responses from the librarians of AMU and BHU confirmed the number as 10 and 8 respectively whereas the librarians of ALU and BBAU have not responded. However, when asked as to how many people perform book selection in the library system, the response changed. Two libraries i.e. AMU and BHU have 7 and 5 selectors respectively; Whereas ALU and BBAU have opted for not responded. Librarians of AMU and BHU showed that the selectors report to them while ALU and BBRAU have not responded.

Table 39. Selection Criteria Adopted by the Librarians for Purchasing Textbooks

Selection Criteria	*AMU*	*BHU*	*ALU*	*BBAU*	*Total Population 100%*
Lists given by Faculty members	Y	Y	Y	Y	100
Lists given by students	Y	Y	Y	Y	100
Recommended by Department	Y	Y	Y	Y	100
Themselves	Y	Y	Y	Y	100
Other	—	—	—	—	

Source: Questionnaire – B, Question No. 11

In the quest to find out how librarians or libraries select text books for purchases. All the responses from the central university libraries were almost the same as that of selecting text books for purchasing. They consider lists given by faculty members, students, recommended by respective departments and at times themselves too.

Table 40. Functions of Collection Development Committee

What is the function of this committee	*AMU*	*BHU*	*ALU*	*BBAU*	*Total Population 100%*
Advisory	—	—	—	—	
Policy making	Y	Y	—	—	50
Decision making	—	—	—	—	

Source : Questionnaire – B, Question No. 13

Another question attempted to gauge whether libraries have any collection development committee. All the librarians queried stated that their libraries have no collection development committees. The author observes that instead of collection development committee the Indian University libraries have library committees and purchase committees, which have taken the responsibility of collection development as well. And most of the libraries have combined functions which focus on the advisory as well as policy making functions. The university libraries have advisory committees. The members of library committee are generally all Deans, all Heads of Department, library administrators and very few teaching members. Most of the members of library committee are nominated by the head of the institution.

In a synonymous question as to whom serves on this committee, librarians of AMU and BHU responded that generally the librarian serves on this committee. The librarians of ALU and BBAU did not offer any response to this question.

Table 41. Authorities on the Committee

Who Serves on	*AMU*	*BHU*	*ALU*	*BBAU*	*Total Population 100%*
This Committee					
Librarian	Y	Y	—	—	50
Collection development In-charge	—	—	—	—	
Selectors/ Bibliographers	—	—	—	—	
Acquisition Librarian	—	—	—	—	
Departmental Heads	—	—	—	—	
Faculty Members	—	—	—	—	
Other (Please specify)	—	—	—	—	

Source: Questionnaire – B, Question No. 14

In another question as to how be the members of this committee were selected, the librarian of BHU responded that selection is being based on nomination whereas the others did not respond.

Table 42. Faculty Members Control on Selection of Materials

Does Faculty Members have control in the following areas	*Rank 1*	*Rank 2*	*Rank 3*	*Rank* Weightage*
Selection of materials	3	1	0	11
Allocation of funds	0	1	3	5
Expenditure of funds	1	2	1	8

Source: Questionnaire – B, Question No. 16

At one time teaching faculty had a very strong role to play in the development of the collection, it seemed appropriate to examine whether or not the library had managed to regain control. Three factors were chosen as being indicative of the role of faculty may have. The librarians were asked to rank the amount of control on a scale from 0 to 5, and 5 being complete control. A summary of the responses is manifested in Table-42. It is discernible from the table that no librarian believes that faculty has complete control of any of these collection development activities. Almost all respondents noted that they solicit advice from faculty. They also indicated that the library often intimates faculty of selection decisions and solicits input from them. In all four cases it was mentioned that faculty, in the respective departments have control over a portion of the funds that are used to purchase library materials for their departmental library.

In terms of full responsibility over selection of library materials and allocation of budget, the librarians of BHU and BBAU communicated that they have full responsibility for selection, whereas the remaining librarians of AMU and ALU have denied this context. In AMU and ALU it comes under the purview of library committee. In terms of full responsibility for allocation of budget, the librarians of AMU and BBAU have negated and the librarians of BHU and ALU have not responded. The author feels that in Indian libraries, allocation of funds comes under the purchase committee and the acquisition department in the sphere of expenditure.

Regarding involvement of librarians and acquisition - in charge in overall library policy, all the librarians have made it known that they do not have a voice in such matters. Almost all the collection Development–In-charge of central university libraries negated their role in determining overall policy.

There were two more questions which tried to determine if there have been substantial trends regarding changes in collection development organizational pattern. (Table-43) There has been increasing awareness among university librarians as regards scope of collection development. Information Technology (IT) and IT enabled services came into existence and influence the services in libraries. In response to whether or not there had been change in structure or organizational pattern of collection

Table 43. Reasons for Change in the Structure of the Collection Development Unit

Reasons for Change	*AMU*	*BHU*	*ALU*	*BBAU*	*Total Population 100%*
To accommodate changes brought about by computerization.	Y	Y	Y	—	75
Shifting priorities within the library.	—	—	Y	—	25
To accommodate changes in personnel.	—	—	—	—	
Change in top-level administration.	—	—	Y	Y	50
Other	—	—	—	—	

Source: Questionnaire – B, Question No. 21

development unit, the librarians of AMU, BHU, and ALU answered in the affirmative. They confirmed that they accommodate changes by adopting computerization. The responses under 'change in top level administration' have been given by newly centralized university librarians i.e., ALU and BBAU while the librarian of ALU also communicated that organizational placement of collection development is due to satisfying priorities within the library.

The changes made seem to have been positive ones. Consequently, it was somewhat disconcerting to discover that BHU, ALU and BBAU of the responding collection development In-charge (Acquisition Librarian) are dissatisfied with the mode of organized collection development. Only AMU gave affirmative response to this question.

It is indeed very difficult to know whether or not the final question regarding anticipated changes can lead one to be optimistic about the future. All the librarians anticipate changes in their organizational pattern, which it is hoped will improve the prevailing situation.

CONCLUSION

In all these libraries the collection development in-charge (usually the acquisition librarian) are not administratively in-charge of collection development. AMU and BHU have a collection development in-charge i.e. acquisition librarian. Acquisition librarian reports to university librarian and university librarian report to Registrar in all the libraries. All the librarians select text books for purchase, they consider lists given by faculty members, students, and recommended by the departments. AMU and BHU collection development librarians have control over personnel. Most of the librarians serve on the committees like purchase committee, book selection committee and other library committees. In BHU the committee members are selected through nomination. However, no librarians have complete control on collection development activities. In the selection of documents they solicit advice from faculty. The librarians have control over a portion of funds. The acquisition librarians (collection development In-charge) of libraries have no voice in such matters. Acquisition Librarian (Collection Development In-charge) or librarians of BHU, ALU and BBAU are dissatisfied with the way their libraries have organized collection development.

5

Information Technology (IT) Application in University Libraries

In an era of globalization the role and the importance of IT is considered to be significant and vital to integrate the economies, businesses, trade and dissemination of knowledge by enlarging the societies globally. The IT industries are playing the role of torch bearer by generating, processing, disseminating and transmitting information. In order to make and integrate the Indian libraries with global libraries, the application and usage of IT is of paramount significance. Almost all over the world, libraries are making all out efforts to make use of IT and its applications for developing collection and policy pertaining to organization. The concept that is now gaining currency is collection development. In the IT based environment in the libraries they are dealing with growth of buildings and expansion of libraries, selection and acquisition of library materials. Now, the collection development policy is being acknowledged to be wider and larger including the policies a pertinent to housing, preservation, storage, weeding and discarding of stack. The entire focus of collection development management is now on the systematic maintenance and management of existing library's collection.

Against this backdrop the author has framed a questionnaire to know and to determine the extent of use and application of IT in the management of collection development its organization and service.

Question were drawn up relating to the availability of different kinds of computers and their usage, and the use of CD drives, OPAC terminals and Networks (Table 44). All the librarians communicated that they have no minicomputer whereas personal computers are available in all libraries. The total number of PCs in AMU is 87; BHU-100, ALU-35 and BBAU - 6.

Table 44. Availability of Computers, Drivers, OPAC, Network

Why were these changes made?	*Yes*				*No*				*Total Population 100%*	
	AMU	*BHU*	*ALU*	*BBAU*	*AMU*	*BHU*	*ALU*	*BBAU*	*Yes*	*No*
Mini Computer	—	—	—	—	N	N	N	N	0	100
No. of personal computers	87	100	35	06	—	—	—	—		
CD Drives	Y	Y	Y	—	—	—	—	N	75	25
OPAC Terminals	Y	—	—	—	—	N	N	N	25	75
Computer Network	Y	Y	Y	—	—	—	—	N	75	25
CD Network	—	Y	Y	—	N	—	—	N	50	50

Source: Questionnaire – C, Question No. 1

The librarians of AMU, BHU and ALU have confirmed having CD Drives whereas BBAU has no such kind of facility. Online Public Access Catalogue terminals are available in AMU only whereas in BHU, ALU and BBAU there are no OPAC terminals. Computer networking is available in AMU, BHU and ALU whereas BBAU has none. The librarians of BHU and ALU confirmed that they have CD-network also.

Table 45. Operating System Used in Libraries

Operating System	*Yes*				*No*				*Total Population 100%*	
	AMU	*BHU*	*ALU*	*BBAU*	*AMU*	*BHU*	*ALU*	*BBAU*	*Yes*	*No*
MS DOS	Y	—	—	—	—	N	N	N	25	75
UNIX	—	—	—	—	N	N	N	N	0	100
Windows	Y	Y	Y	Y	—	—	—	—	100	0

Source: Questionnaire – C, Question No. 2

Another question was framed by the author to examine the operating system used by the libraries. It is observed that all the respondents have confirmed that they are using Windows. Whereas AMU is exceptional which uses MS-DOS also. UNIX operating system has not been used by any of these libraries.

Table 46. Word Processor Used in Libraries

Word Processor Used in Libraries	*Yes*				*No*				*Total Population 100%*	
	AMU	*BHU*	*ALU*	*BBAU*	*AMU*	*BHU*	*ALU*	*BBAU*	*Yes*	*No*
Word Perfect	—	—	—	—	N	N	N	N	0	100
Word Star	—	—	—	—	N	N	N	N	0	100
MS Word	Y	Y	Y	Y	—	—	—	—	100	0
AmiPro	—	—	—	—	N	N	N	N	0	100

Source: Questionnaire – C, Question No. 3

A question was framed to know whether word processor was used by the libraries. All the librarians have corroborated that they use only MS-Word whereas Word Perfect, Word Star, AmiPro are not used by any library.

AMU, BHU and ALU are found to use the library software for maintaining collection and services and other functions the librarians of AMU, BHU and ALU also demonstrate that they are using library software i.e., Libsys by AMU and ALU and Genlib by BHU.

Table 47. Computerized Library Operations

Computerized Library Operations	*Yes*				*No*				*Total Population 100%*	
	AMU	*BHU*	*ALU*	*BBAU*	*AMU*	*BHU*	*ALU*	*BBAU*	*Yes*	*No*
Acquisition	Y	—	—	—	—	N	N	N	25	75
Cataloguing	Y	Y	Y	—	—	—	—	N	75	25
Circulation	Y	—	—	—	—	N	N	N	25	75
OPAC	Y	—	—	—	—	N	N	N	25	75
Retrospective Conv.	Y	Y	Y	—	—	—	—	N	75	25
Serials Control	Y	—	—	—	—	N	N	N	25	75
Budgeting	—	—	—	—	N	N	N	N	0	100
Statistical Report	—	—	—	—	N	N	N	N	0	100

Source: Questionnaire – C, Question No. 5

Regarding computerized library operations, BHU, ALU and BBAU answered that Acquisition, Circulation, OPAC, and Serial control are not used. AMU, BHU and ALU have echoed that cataloging and retrospective conversion is being made use of. For Budgeting and statistical reports computer are not used by any of these libraries. The librarians have also reported that they are implementing library automation in phases (Table-47).

Table 48. Computerized Facilities Offered to Users

Computerized Library Operations	*Yes*				*No*				*Total Population 100%*	
	AMU	*BHU*	*ALU*	*BBAU*	*AMU*	*BHU*	*ALU*	*BBAU*	*Yes*	*No*
Computers provided to users	Y	Y	Y	-	-	-	-	N	75	25
OPAC	Y	-	-	-	-	N	N	N	25	75
CD-ROM Search	-	Y	Y	-	N	-	-	N	50	50
Internet	Y	Y	Y	-	-	-	-	N	75	25
Online search	Y	Y	Y	-	-	-	-	N	75	25
E-mail	Y	Y	Y	-	-	-	-	N	75	25

Source: Questionnaire – C, Question No. 7

A question was also served with regard to computerized facility offered to the users (Table-48). The libraries of AMU, BHU and ALU provide computerized facility to the users. The OPAC facility is being provided by only AMU. ALU, BHU and BBAU do not provide OPAC facility. As regards providing CD-ROM search facility to users ALU and BHU echoed that they cater to this service and AMU and BBAU denied providing CD-ROM search facility .Internet, Online search and E-mail services are provided by the libraries of AMU, BHU and ALU. BBAU is the lone university library which is not providing this facility to user's.

Table 49. Digitization of Collection

Digitization of Collection	*% of*				*SW Used*			
	AMU	*BHU*	*ALU*	*BBAU*	*AMU*	*BHU*	*ALU*	*BBAU*
Books	-	-	50	-	-	-	-	-
Theses	-	-	-	-	-	-	-	-
Manuscripts	100	100	-	-	Adobe-7	-	-	-
Other (please specify)	15	10	-	-	-	-	-	-

Source: Questionnaire – C, Question No. 8.2

A question was devised by the author to enquire about the digitization of collection and networking development in these libraries. The answer received from the librarians was divergent (Table-49). It is interesting to observe that only ALU has digitized about 50% of its collection of books. Manuscripts have been digitized100% in AMU and BHU, whereas other forms of documents that are pages from rare journals have been digitized AMU and BHU. The software used in digitization at AMU was Adobe-7.

The author has designed two questions as regards to the type of Internet connection used in the library and in the participation of networks by them at National Level (Tables 50 and 51). All the respondents are found to have used leased line for internet connectivity in their libraries. AMU, BHU and ALU are the members of INFLIBNET. BHU and ALU are also participating in DELNET.

Table 50. Type of Internet Connection Used in the Library

Type of Internet connection	*Yes*				*No*				*Total Population 100%*	
	AMU	*BHU*	*ALU*	*BBAU*	*AMU*	*BHU*	*ALU*	*BRAU*	*Yes*	*No*
Leased	Y	Y	Y	Y	—	—	—	—	100	0
Dial-up	—	—	—	—	N	N	N	N	0	100
VSAT	—	—	—	—	N	N	N	N	0	100
ISDN	—	—	—	—	N	N	N	N	0	100
Radio Modem	—	—	—	—	N	N	N	N	0	100

Source: Questionnaire – C, Question No. 8.3

Table 51. Membership of Networks

Member of networks	*Yes*				*No*				*Total Population 100%*	
	AMU	*BHU*	*ALU*	*BBAU*	*AMU*	*BHU*	*ALU*	*BBAU*	*Yes*	*No*
Capital inflibnet	Y	Y	Y	—	—	—	—	N	75	25
DELNET	—	Y	Y	—	N	—	—	N	50	50
ERNET	—	—	—	—	N	N	N	N	0	100
NICNET	—	—	—	—	N	N	N	N	0	100
INET	—	—	—	—	N	N	N	N	0	100

Source: Questionnaire – C, Question No. 8.4

CONCLUSION

It is found from analysis so far as the IT Enabled services are concerned only AMU has OPAC terminals. AMU, BHU and ALU have computer networking. Only BHU and ALU have CD-network. AMU and ALU are using Libsys software and BHU are using Genlib for maintaining their collection management and service. The computerized library operations for Acquisition, Circulation, OPAC and Serial Control are not used by BHU, ALU and BBAU. In AMU, BHU and ALU cataloging and retrospective conversion are being made use of. Budgeting and statistical report modules are not used by any library. Only ALU has digitized half of its collection. AMU and BHU have been digitized all their manuscripts collection. They have also digitized certain pages from rare journals. AMU, BHU and ALU are the members of INFLIBNET where as BHU and ALU are also the members of DELNET.

6

Users' Assessment of Library Services

A library is an important and integral component of any high quality academic institution. The university libraries are no exception to this. The users must have full knowledge about the services of the library to fulfill their needs in order to properly exploit library resources. The users' satisfaction is considered to be reliable criterion for determining effectiveness of the library. It helps the library to meet its users' information needs in an effective way by providing standard and suitable library services needed by them. Adequacy of collections is one of the important factors that determine the effectiveness of any library in meeting the information needs of its users. A user oriented approach has been found to be more suitable for measuring library effectiveness. For this purpose, users' survey is a very useful tool as it studies the relationship that exists between the library and the users. The study of the users' opinions is regarded as the means of systematic study of users' behavior in using and assessing the library services available to them. The present study is undertaken by the author to find out the availability of different types of collection, facilities, services and to know how far the university libraries are able to fulfill the information needs of its faculty members', research scholars' and students' in the support of their teaching, research and academic activities.

To find out users' assessment as regards collection development its organization and services, questionnaire and interview-based survey was designed for data collection. This technique is chosen as it is helpful to gather information from scattered population. Several studies on related topics have also been consulted and their tools and techniques have been appropriately used. Personal interviews were also conducted with some respondents. The purpose of these interviews was to seek clarifications for certain trends emerging as a result of data analysis and to seek the opinion of respondents on the performance of library.

An attempt was made to investigate the purpose of visit to the library by the different categories of users. It is indicative from the table that the faculty members in AMU occasionally visit the library for issue and return of the documents (See Table-1). However, 72.73% of respondents among faculty members form BHU visit the library for the Issue and returns of the documents. 50% and 34% faculty members of ALU and BBAU respectively visit the library for the Issue and returns of the documents. The faculty members from BBAU visits library for casual/leisure reading (100%), followed by BHU (35.91%), AMU (17.2%) and ALU (6.25%) respectively. The responses of faculty members show that 36.82% of BHU visit library for reading the prescribed text books followed by AMU (1.1%). In order to prepare for classroom instructions 50% respondents of ALU, 30% from BHU and BBAU and 30.9% from AMU are found to be visiting the library. Highest member of respondents visit the library to consult documents for research purpose are from BHU, followed by ALU and AMU. It shows that BHU and ALU libraries are providing better documents for research. Furthermore, author found out from verbal responses that faculty members from AMU get better research and teaching materials from their departmental seminar libraries.

The table also provides responses of research scholars pertaining to the purpose of visit to the library. 80.52% respondents from BHU visit the library for Issues and return of documents, followed by AMU, BBAU, and ALU respectively. This comparison shows that two old central universities are providing better infrastructural support to their research scholars. Table further indicates that research scholars from BBAU are fully dependent on the library to consult documents for research purpose whereas 91.3% research scholars of AMU visit library to consult documents for research purpose followed by BHU and ALU. The researcher feels that research scholars from AMU, BHU and ALU are having some alternative source of information for research purposes as well.

The responses of the students pertaining to the purpose of visit to the library are also shown in the table. Majority of the students from BHU visit library for issue and return of the documents, followed by AMU (64.9%), ALU (44.67%) and BBAU (28.57%) respectively. This shows that BHU and AMUs circulation section is better equipped than other two universities. For reading the prescribed text books 75.9% of the students from AMU, followed by BHU (66.57%), ALU (49.33%) and BBAU (30.36%) respectively visit the library indicating that the textual sections of two old centralized universities are better than the other two. In order to prepare for competitive examination 84.64% students from BHU, 74.6% from ALU, 44.81% from AMU and 34.82% from BBRAU visit the library.

The author feels that BHU and ALU are providing good environment for competitive study within the library premises. The AMU is also having a separate coaching and guidance cell for competitive study.

In Table 2 an attempt was made to show the comparative statistics relating to satisfaction with library infrastructure and facilities. It is discernible from table that majority of faculty members from AMU and BHU are satisfied with the provision of separate reading rooms whereas faculty members of the ALU and the BBRAU show their

Table 1. Purpose of Visit to Library (Usefulness and Utility of Library)

Purpose of Visit to Library	*Faculty Members (Yes %)*				*Research Scholars (Yes %)*				*Students (Yes %)*			
	AMU	*BHU*	*ALU*	*BBAU*	*AMU*	*BHU*	*ALU*	*BBAU*	*AMU*	*BHU*	*ALU*	*BBAU*
For Issue/Return of the documents.	13.0	72.73	34.38	50	77.2	80.52	41.03	50	64.9	78.92	44.67	28.57
For casual/leisure reading	17.2	35.91	6.25	100	29.3	59.74	29.49	75	19.5	35.24	32.67	40.18
For reading the prescribed text-books	1.1	36.82	0.00	0	88.0	61.04	15.38	25	75.9	66.57	59.33	30.36
To prepare for classroom instructions	30.9	30.00	50.00	30	5.4	11.69	2.56	0	1.7	0.00	0.67	37.50
To consult documents for research purpose	28.2	95.91	40.63	10	91.3	88.31	57.69	100	0.6	29.52	0.00	28.57
To study for competitive examinations	0.0	5.45	0.00	0	58.7	46.75	46.15	25	44.8	84.64	74.67	34.82
Any other	0.0		0.00	0	0.0	0.00	0.00	0	0.0	0.00	0.00	0.00

Source : Compiled from Users' Survey

dissatisfaction with library infrastructure and facilities. Provision of reading tables in AMU library is the best among all libraries of the universities under reference.

Responses of the research scholars regarding the satisfaction with library infrastructure and facilities are also provided in this table, which shows that AMU is having separate reading rooms for different categories of students with suitable reading tables. BHU is also found to be providing separate rooms with adequate provision of reading tables. However, responses of Research scholars reveal that the ALU and the BBAU libraries are not providing adequate separate reading rooms and reading tables. The researcher feels that due to the lack of funds newly centralized universities are unable to provide good library infrastructure and facilities to research scholars. Responses of students with regard to satisfaction with library infrastructure and facilities are also presented in the table. Most of the respondents from AMU and BHU have expressed their satisfaction with the available infrastructure.

Table 3 presents responses pertaining to satisfaction with reading room facilities in terms of adequacy of light, overall serenity of atmosphere, opening hours of reading rooms and availability of books for on the spot reading. In terms of adequacy of lights the BHU holds the first position as per the response of the faculty members, followed by the others. Response of the faculty members of BBRAU shows that overall serenity of atmosphere is the best among the libraries of universities under review. In terms of opening hours of reading rooms majority of faculty members of AMU are satisfied. However, the satisfaction level of the majority of faculty members of BHU, ALU and BBAU is low which shows dissatisfaction. Satisfaction in terms of availability of books for on the spot reading shows a very discouraging account of all the libraries under study.

Majority of the research scholars from AMU and BHU are satisfied with adequacy of lights, and overall serenity of atmosphere. The research scholars from AMU are satisfied with the opening of reading rooms whereas, only 49.35%

research scholars from BHU are satisfied with the opening of reading rooms. BBRAU's performance in terms of adequacy of lights, overall serenity of atmosphere and opening of reading rooms is better than that of the ALU. Furthermore, table gives an account of responses of students regarding satisfaction with reading room facilities. Majority of the students from AMU are satisfied with the reading room facilities, 64.16% of the students from BHU are satisfied with adequacy of lights and 59.64% of the students are satisfied with the reading room facilities. Only 53.92% students from BHU have shown satisfaction with opening of reading rooms. Responses of students from ALU and BBAU show that there are poor reading room facilities in their libraries. From the discussions it can be inferred that the reading room facilities in old centralized universities are better than the newly centralized universities.

Table 4 presents responses collected from faculty members, research scholars and the students regarding satisfaction with the number of borrower cards and outside reading room facilities. Majority of faculty members form AMU and BHU are satisfied with number of cards issued, number of book issued on each card and the loan period. However, faculty members from ALU and BBAU are not satisfied with the number of cards and outside reading facilities provided by their libraries. The responses from the research scholars towards the number of borrower cards issued show that 77.92% research scholars from BHU, followed by 66.67% form BBAU, 58.7% from AMU and 43.59% from ALU are satisfied. 75% respondents among research scholars of BBAU are satisfied with the number of book issued on each card, followed by BHU; AMU and ALU respectively.

The responses of students, another important segment of library users, are also presented in this table. It shows that majority of the students of BHU are satisfied with the number of borrower cards and outside reading facilities. 75.90% of the respondents from AMU, 54.46% from BBAU and 29.33% from ALU are satisfied with the number of books issued. Less

Table 2. Satisfaction with Library Infrastructure and Facilities (Degree of Library Resources and Availability of Infrastructure)

Satisfied with the library Infrastructure and Facilities	*Faculty Members (Yes %)*				*Research Scholars (Yes %)*				*Students (Yes %)*			
	AMU	*BHU*	*ALU*	*BBAU*	*AMU*	*BHU*	*ALU*	*BBAU*	*AMU*	*BHU*	*ALU*	*BBAU*
Provision of separate reading rooms.	65.6	62.73	15.63	20	78.3	63.64	29.49	25	52.3	40.06	22.67	27.68
Provision of reading tables.	61.5	45.91	21.88	30	68.5	79.22	35.90	25	64.4	64.46	15.33	36.61

Source : Compiled from Users' Survey

Table 3. Satisfaction with Reading Room Facilities (Adequacy of Infrastructural Facilities)

Satisfaction with reading room facilities in terms of	*Faculty Members (Yes %)*				*Research Scholars (Yes %)*				*Students (Yes %)*			
	AMU	*BHU*	*ALU*	*BBAU*	*AMU*	*BHU*	*ALU*	*BBAU*	*AMU*	*BHU*	*ALU*	*BBAU*
Adequacy of lights	46.9	64.55	37.50	40	88.0	77.92	17.95	50	77.0	64.16	14.00	57.14
Overall serenity of atmosphere	22.5	48.18	18.75	50	58.7	79.22	23.08	50	68.4	59.64	8.00	30.36
Opening of reading rooms.	85.1	45.91	28.13	30	78.3	49.35	26.92	50	94.3	53.92	15.33	40.18
Availability of books for on the spot Reading	15.6	9.55	25.00	40	39.1	37.66	5.13	16.667	52.3	35.54	1.33	20.54

Source: Compiled from Users' Survey

Table 4. Satisfaction with Number of Cards and Outside Reading Facilities (Library Function Efficiency and Effectiveness)

Content with the out side reading facilities	*Faculty Members (Yes %)*				*Research Scholars (Yes %)*				*Students (Yes %)*			
	AMU	*BHU*	*ALU*	*BBAU*	*AMU*	*BHU*	*ALU*	*BBAU*	*AMU*	*BHU*	*ALU*	*BBAU*
Number of cards issued.	81.3	90.45	40.63	40	58.7	77.92	43.59	66.667	59.8	62.65	28.67	58.93
No. of book issued on each card.	79.8	91.36	37.50	50	55.4	62.34	39.74	75	75.9	63.55	29.33	54.46
Loan period of documents.	80.9	83.18	18.75	30	39.1	31.17	26.92	25	43.7	75.90	19.33	20.54

Source : Compiled from Users' Survey

Table 5. Users' Response about the Use of Catalogue (Functional Effectiveness)

Categories of Catalogue	*Faculty Members (Yes %)*				*Research Scholars (Yes %)*				*Students (Yes %)*			
	AMU	*BHU*	*ALU*	*BBAU*	*AMU*	*BHU*	*ALU*	*BBAU*	*AMU*	*BHU*	*ALU*	*BBAU*
Card catalogue	1.5	100.00	100.00	100.00	2.2	100.00	100.00	100.00	5.2	100.00	100.00	100.00
Online Public Access Catalogue	96.2	00.00	0.00	0.00	19.6	00.00	0.00	0.00	75.9	00.00	0.00	0.00
Both	2.3	0000	0.00	0.00	78.3	0000	0.00	0.00	17.8	0000	0.00	0.00

Source : Compiled From Users' Survey

than 60% students from AMU and BBAU are satisfied with the number of card issued by the library.

The author therefore, feels that AMU and BHU give more focus on providing borrowers card and outside reading facilities to the faculty members. Responses of the research scholars and students from AMU and BHU show average satisfaction with regard to the number of borrower cards and outside reading facilities.

Responses from the faculty members, research scholars and the students towards the use of catalogue are presented in Table 5. All the respondents from BHU, ALU and BBAU show that they are 100% dependent on card catalogue. Response of the faculty members and students of AMU present the fact that majority of them uses Online Public Access Catalogue, whereas research scholars are using OPAC as well as card catalogue facilities. The author during investigation found that except AMU, no other university library are not providing OPAC faculty to its users.

In Table-6 users' participation in collection development is shown. Majority of faculty members from AMU, BHU and BBAU actively participate in collection development. There is negligible participation of the faculty members in ALU in collection development. Response of the research scholars and the students present the facts that there is hardly any participation from the research scholars and the students in collection development. Therefore author feels that university authorities are relying highly on the advice of the faculty members in collection development.

The response of the faculty members, research scholars and the students towards the method of their participation in collection development are presented in Table-7. Majority of the respondents among the AMU faculty members participate in collection development by pointing out the weaknesses of the collection of the particular subject. According the survey 43.5% faculty members of AMU participate in collection development through formal requisitions and suggestions. Response of faculty members

Table 6. Users' Participation in Collection Building

Participation in Building Collection	*Faculty Members(Yes %)*				*Research Scholars(Yes %)*				*Students(Yes %)*			
	AMU	*BHU*	*ALU*	*BBAU*	*AMU*	*BHU*	*ALU*	*BBAU*	*AMU*	*BHU*	*ALU*	*BBAU*
Yes	67.9	73.18	37.50	70	39.1	28.57	5.13	25.00	12.1	6.33	6.00	0.00
No	8.8	25.45	34.38	30	58.7	66.23	52.56	66.67	77.0	68.37	28.00	0.00
No Response	23.3	1.36	28.13	0	2.2	5.19	42.31	8.33	10.9	25.30	66.00	100.00

Source: Compiled From Users' Survey

Table 7. Method of Participation in Collection Building (Figure in Parenthesis is Percentage)

Method of Participation	*Faculty Members (Yes %)*				*Research Scholars (Yes %)*				*Students (Yes %)*			
	AMU	*BHU*	*ALU*	*BBAU*	*AMU*	*BHU*	*ALU*	*BBAU*	*AMU*	*BHU*	*ALU*	*BBAU*
As a member of document selection committee	10.7	34.55	6.25	—	0.00	0.00	0.00	—	0.00	0.30	0.00	0.00
As a subject specialist, when asked to render help in document selection	34.0	55.00	18.75	40	5.43	24.68	3.85	—	1.15	2.71	0.00	0.00
Through formal requisition and suggestion	43.5	45.91	56.25.	40	28.6	10.39	30.77	—	27.9	2.41	1.33	38.39
By pointing out the weakness of the collection of the particular subject	75.2	33.18	43.75	—	45.0	38.96	20.51	—	43.3	3.92	2.67	—
By any other method	0.0	0.00	0.00	—	0.00	0.00		—	0.0	0.00		—

Source: Compiled From Users' Survey

of BHU presents more balanced participation in collection development. Almost 56.2% faculty members of ALU participate in collection development through formal requisitions and suggestions followed by 43.75% by pointing out the weakness of the collection of particular subject, 18.75% as subject specialists. Only 6.25% faculty members ALU, 34.55% of BHU and 10.7% of AMU participate in collection development as a member of book selection committee. Response of research scholars and students present a negligible participation in collection development. Lack of participation from the research scholars and the students indicates that all the libraries are using the experience of the faculty members in collection development.

It has been, therefore, understood that the student's representation in the libraries give better chance to participate in the collection building. However they feel that it has not been used by the libraries in proper manner. The majority of the users suggest formally for new subscriptions and also point out the pressing needs for participation through the method of oral and written communication. Other than the three methods of participation i.e. students representation, formal suggestion, participation through method of oral and written, the faculty members participate on the basis of their subject expertise in the concerned fields and it has been ranked as third method of collection development.

The users in BBAU are not at all using the method of pointing out the weaknesses and there appears to be absence of students' representation in the selection. It is evident that in case of AMU all the four methods are largely utilized by the different users as and when required.

Response collected from the faculty members, research scholars and the students regarding frequency of making suggestions for the procurement of materials are represented in Table-8. It is found that 50.4% faculty members of AMU occasionally make suggestions for procurement of materials for the library, whereas 30.2% among faculty members of AMU frequently make suggestions for procurement of materials. 36.82% BHU faculty members frequently make suggestions whereas only 6.25% faculty members of ALU and 20% of BBAU respectively frequently make suggestions.

Response of the research scholars and the students failed to show any particular trend at which they make suggestions for procurement of materials for the library. The author feels that the librarians do not encourage and entertain suggestions for the procurement of materials from the research scholars and the students. This is ascribed to lack of trust of university library authorities in the ability of research scholar and the students for the suggestions. Furthermore, researcher feels that the research scholars and the students are also hesitant in giving suggestions due mainly to lack of awareness.

The Table No.-9 presents the response towards users' suggestions for procuring reading materials in libraries. It is seen that 61.5% of the faculty members of AMU suggested that the response of library authorities is positive in accommodating their suggestions for procuring reading materials. Whereas, 67.73% faculty members of BHU responded that library authorities took their suggestions for procuring reading materials positively. In case of ALU, the faculty members opined that library attitude is negative in considering their suggestions. While 40% faculty members of BBAU suggest that the library authorities are fair in considering their suggestions. Response of research scholars from AMU and BHU gave a mixed opinion. The tabular facts are indicative that 50% of the research scholars of AMU feel that the library is fair towards their suggestions. The responses of research scholars from BHU suggest that 40.26% is positive for the procuring reading material. In case of ALU and BBAU, majority of the respondents consented that the library response towards uses suggestions for procuring reading materials is negative.

The response of the students of AMU reveals that in majority of the cases library response is positive and fair. In case of BHU, ALU and BBAU the majority of the students formed their opinion that library response towards users

Table 8. Frequency to Make Suggestions for Procurement of Materials
(Figure in Parenthesis is Percentage)

Frequency of at which you make suggestions for procurement of materials for the library	*Faculty Members (Yes%)*				*Research Scholar (Yes%)*				*Students (Yes%)*			
	AMU	*BHU*	*ALU*	*BBAU*	*AMU*	*BHU*	*ALU*	*BBAU*	*AMU*	*BHU*	*ALU*	*BBAU*
Frequently	30.2	36.82	6.25	20	29.3	16.88	1.28	25.00	19.5	14.46	0.67	1.79
Rarely	16.4	18.64	28.13	40	2.2	25.97	50.00	25.00	44.8	42.47	38.00	54.46
Occasionally	50.4	17.73	43.75	30	39.1	9.09	28.21	41.67	12.6	23.80	3.33	18.75
Never	3.1	26.82	21.88	10	29.3	44.16	20.51	8.33	23.0	19.28	58.00	25.00

Source : Compiled From Users' Survey

Table 9. Library Response towards Users' Suggestions for Procuring Reading Materials

Response of the library towards users' suggestions for procuring reading materials	*Faculty Members(Yes%)*				*Research Scholars (Yes%)*				*Students (Yes%)*			
	AMU	*BHU*	*ALU*	*BBAU*	*AMU*	*BHU*	*ALU*	*BBAU*	*AMU*	*BHU*	*ALU*	*BBAU*
Positive	61.5	67.73	34.38	30	26.1	40.26	16.67	8.33	30.5	21.39	15.33	19.64
Negative	11.1	25.00	56.25	30	23.9	36.36	78.21	75.00	38.5	64.16	79.33	73.21
Fair	27.5	7.27	9.38	40	50.0	23.38	5.13	16.67	31.0	14.46	5.33	7.14

Source : Compiled From Users' Survey

suggestions for procuring reading material is negative. The author, therefore, feels that in case of old central universities suggestions from the users are welcome by the library authorities whereas the attitude of newly centralized libraries towards users' suggestion is negative. Furthermore, in case of newly centralized universities there is a lack of awareness among the staff and users about the various functional areas of collection development.

In Table-10 the response of the users regarding their awareness about the various library services. It is recognized from the table that majority of the respondents among the faculty members, research scholars and the students are aware about the lending and circulation services except the students of BBAU. Majority of the faculty members and research scholar are aware about inter -library loan, reference and bibliographic services. However, among the students there is lack of awareness about the inter -library loan. 69.5% and 67.17% students of AMU and BHU are aware about the reference services, whereas, the response of the students from ALU and BBAU show that only few students are aware about reference service. A large percentage of users among faculty members and research scholars of AMU and BHU have knowledge about Current Awareness Service (CAS). The response also shows that a handful of faculty members and research scholars of ALU and BBAU are aware about CAS. Among the students most of them are not aware about CAS. In case of Selective Dissemination of Information (SDI) majority of the respondents from all the categories show their lack of awareness. Response regarding the reprographic services reveals that the majority of them are well aware about this service. 59.38% respondents among faculty members of ALU, 50% of BBAU are aware about the translation services also. Among other respondents 66.3% research scholars of AMU have knowledge of translation services. Comparative responses presented in the table indicates that majority of the respondents are aware about on-line services. In case of Indexing and Abstracting services, faculty members of BHU and BBAU are more aware than the AMU and ALU. Whereas,

Table 10. Users Awareness about the Various Library Services

Users Awareness of Services	*Faculty Members (Yes%)*				*Research Scholars (yes%)*				*Students (Yes%)*			
	AMU	*BHU*	*ALU*	*BBAU*	*AMU*	*BHU*	*ALU*	*BBAU*	*AMU*	*BHU*	*ALU*	*BBAU*
Lending circulation services	88.2	93.18	90.63	100	84.8	85.71	82.05	75	73.6	74.70	74.67	29.46
Inter Library loan	80.5	90.45	53.13	80	78.3	84.42	50.00	50	35.1	33.73	24.67	10.71
Reference service	81.3	95.91	43.75	70	72.8	75.32	53.85	58.333	69.5	67.17	28.67	11.61
Bibliographical services	81.7	92.73	40.63	80	71.7	70.13	52.56	66.667	41.4	45.78	17.33	18.75
CAS	67.9	93.18	6.25	10	67.4	66.23	29.49	16.667	23.6	37.05	0.00	0.00
SDI	3.4	2.73	3.13	10	33.7	36.36	2.56	8.3333	0.6	0.00	0.00	0.00
Reprographic Services	100.0	96.36	100.00	90	91.3	87.01	91.03	83.333	96.6	96.69	100.00	68.75
Translation services	23.3	9.09	59.38	50	66.3	24.68	26.92	16.667	0.6	0.60	12.67	5.36
Online service	100.0	99.55	100.00	100	88.0	93.51	88.46	91.667	92.5	96.99	96.00	78.57
Indexing and abstracting services	10.3	70.45	12.50	60	52.2	42.86	26.92	50	10.3	11.14	19.33	3.57

Source : Compiled From Users' Survey

the research scholars of AMU, BHU and BBAU are having better knowledge about Indexing and Abstracting services than research scholars of ALU. Awareness among the students with regard to these services is negligible. The author feels that some of the popular services are also favourite services among the respondents.

In Table-11 statistical information pertaining to use of periodicals by the different categories of respondents under survey was shown. It is evident that 46.9% respondents among the faculty members of AMU use current periodicals whereas 67.9% of them use back volumes of periodicals and, only 26.7% use Indexing and Abstracting periodicals. In case of BHU majority of faculty members use current periodicals as well as back volumes of periodicals. Only 10.45% faculty members utilize Indexing and Abstracting periodicals. Response of faculty members of ALU shows that 37.5% use current periodical and 40.63% use back volumes of periodicals.

From the comparative analysis it is evident in older universities' the users are habituated to use current periodicals and back volumes. However, the students are not frequent users of current periodicals, back volumes periodicals and Indexing and Abstracting periodicals. The author observes that due to lack of funds and high cost of periodicals the newly centralized universities are not able to procure sufficient periodicals, both national and as well as international.

Users' response about provision of different types of reference services provided by library is given in Table-12. A comparative analysis of the response of the users among the faculty members and research scholars show that AMU and BHU are better than ALU in helping in searching documents, help them to use reference sources, and also help them to use bibliographical sources and also in searching for specific information. Among the students' overall performance of BHU is better than AMU and ALU in providing the reference services. The author observes that newly centralized

Table 11. Use of Periodicals by the Users'

Use of Periodicals by the Users'	*Faculty Members (Yes %)*				*Research Scholars (Yes %)*				*Students (Yes %)*			
	AMU	*BHU*	*ALU*	*BBAU*	*AMU*	*BHU*	*ALU*	*BBAU*	*AMU*	*BHU*	*ALU*	*BBAU*
Current periodicals	46.9	72.73	37.50	—	53.3	59.74	29.49	—	12.1	12.35	1.33	—
Back volumes of periodicals	67.9	70.45	40.63	—	44.6	42.86	48.72	—	17.8	6.93	5.33	—
Indexing/Abstracting periodicals	26.7	10.45	3.13	—	30.4	31.17	2.56	—	0.0	3.31	0.67	—

Source : Compiled From Users' Survey

Table 12. Users Response about Provision of Different Types of Reference Service (Service Adequacy and Efficiency)

Does library provide following services	*Faculty Members (Yes %)*				*Research Scholars (Yes %)*				*Students (Yes %)*			
	AMU	*BHU*	*ALU*	*BBAU*	*AMU*	*BHU*	*ALU*	*BBAU*	*AMU*	*BHU*	*ALU*	*BBAU*
Help to search the document	88.2	40.45	6.25	—	39.1	66.23	11.54	—	51.1	35.24	22.67	—
Help to use reference sources	80.9	35.91	12.50	—	58.7	58.44	5.13	—	18.4	26.81	14.00	—
Help to use biblio-graphical sources	58.8	25.45	9.38	—	48.9	32.47	7.69	—	12.1	33.73	14.00	—
Help to search specific information	43.5	45.00	3.13	—	58.7	40.26	10.26	-	6.3	23.19	8.67	—

Source : Compiled From Jsers' Survey

universities are not helping the users much due to lack of adequately trained staff.

In Table-13 users' response about the use of different types of services in the library is presented. The faculty members of AMU mostly use Xeroxing, Internet, online databases, online journals and CAS. Majority of the faculty members of BHU use these services i.e. xeroxing and on-line databases and online journals. The use of other services available in the library is not very common among the BHU faculty members. Comparison of the three universities' faculty members' responses shows that the majority uses Xeroxing, Internet and on-line database and journals in the library.

The comparative study of the responses of research scholar of AMU, BHU and ALU show that majority of them use the three basic services i.e. Xeroxing, Internet and on-line database and journals. The response of the students present that majority of the students use xeroxing service. Only in case of AMU 65.52% students are found to have been using CAS.

The author has observed during his investigation that BBAU is not providing services other than circulation of documents. He fèels that Xeroxing service is popular among all the categories of users. Internet and access to On-line database and journals are the other frequently used services by faculty members and the research scholars. However, students are not allowed to use on-line database service and internet service within the library premises.

CONCLUSION

Many of the earlier studies have suggested that several factors need to be studied to measure library effectiveness. An attempt has been made in the present study which investigated users' perception of library effectiveness with regard to a wide range of factors covering resources, services and activities. It was found that larger libraries with adequate infrastructure facilities, adequate collections were considered

Table 13. Users' Response about the Use of Different Types of Services (Service Effectiveness and Efficiency)

Use of services	*Faculty Members (Yes %)*				*Research Scholars (Yes %)*				*Students (Yes %)*			
	AMU	*BHU*	*ALU*	*BBAU*	*AMU*	*BHU*	*ALU*	*BBAU*	*AMU*	*BHU*	*ALU*	*BBAU*
Bibliographical Services	30.15	31.36	9.38	—	77.17	28.57	16.67	—	33.91	42.47	2.67	—
Xeroxing	53.82	75.45	65.63	—	98.91	79.22	70.51	—	95.98	97.29	74.67	—
Micro Film	11.07	—	0.00	—	10.87	—	0.00	—	6.90	—	0.00	—
SDI	0.00	—	0.00	—	2.17	—	0.00	-	0.00	—	0.00	—
Internet	43.13	25.45	68.75	—	84.78	62.34	29.49	—	0.00	37.05	0.67	—
Online Database, Journal	80.53	80.91	65.63	—	96.74	66.23	26.92	—	0.00	30.42	2.00	—
CAS	75.57	33.18	15.63	—	51.09	40.26	24.36	—	65.52	8.13	0.00	—
CD ROM	0.00	20.00	0.00	—	0.00	50.65	0.00	—	0.00	3.31	0.00	—

Source : Compiled From Users' Survey

more effective. Those Libraries which involve their users in the collection development received a better assessment for effectively meeting the information needs of their users. A relationship was also found between the perception of library effectiveness and the availability of materials, and assistance sought in using library services and its facilities. Those users who visit the library for research purpose and classroom instruction gave better assessments to their library.

On the whole very clear result has emerged from this study. The newly centralized university libraries are found to be in the process of strengthening their infrastructure and facilities. This is vouched by all the categories of the respondents. The universities as well as BHU are not having OPAC. AMU is found to be using both categories of catalogue i.e., card catalogue and OPAC. A good deal of participation by the users in collection development is found by all the universities by the faculty members and research scholars. It is, however, evidently discernible that in a newly centralized university library i.e., BBAU students participation is almost nil. So far as suggestions by the users for procuring reading materials are concerned it is seen that almost all the users of these libraries are found to have made essential suggestions for the purpose. The degree of awareness among the users about various kinds of library services is found to be satisfactory. However, the student respondents of BBAU found to be more satisfied and aware in case of reprographic and on-line services. The degree of use of periodicals, by the users is again satisfactory in case of users of AMU and BHU. The ALU users however, are below the satisfactory and in case of BBAU all the users under the referred categories are found to be lacking the use of these facilities.

7

Strategies for Collection Development

Information forms the basis of appraisal and alignment of thoughts and ideas, and the significance of information to the present society, cannot be ignored. In the post industrial society, economies world-over are moving from being industrial economics to information economies. The use of information technology and IT enabled services (ITES) for transforming knowledge into intelligence has become the fundamental basis of surviving the onslaught of competition and achieving world wide excellence. Consequently, large investments are being made in the IT industry for the purpose of generating, processing and transmitting information. On the question of the impact of IT on library and information work, Slamecka[1] in his study, "Empirical Issues in National Information System Design" in 1985, drew attention to what he considers a significant change required in future system design. Information systems that are presently in use can be handled only by IT professional rather than by general user. Thus, it is quite essential to design information systems which are user friendly and can be handled with ease by common man.

In recent decades, libraries and information centres

have risen to the occasion and are trying to adapt and adopt IT for their operation. Yet, the libraries in India have not kept pace with the pragmatic changes in the field of information technology. It is imperative for libraries to change gear and develop at an accelerated pace to outweigh the bottleneck and hardships of external forces such as economic, political, technical and other internal variables of change. Thus the challenge of change, the pressure of accountability and emergence of enterprise culture are emphasing the fact that the libraries must also change to meet the diversifying needs. Library will have to be flexible enough to adopt to change more rapidly and more creatively.

With the changing environment and the expansion and involvement of IT, a greater need is felt for adapting an approach and philosophy of collection development as there are drastic differences between an IT based and print based environment. However, collection development would still require policies that would govern the acquisition of both electronic resources and traditional forms of documents. There is indeed a challenge to integrate both aspects.

On the basis of a survey of the extensive literature generated on changing collection development patterns, the key issues identified for redefining a collection development policy include: balancing ownership and access; cooperative efforts; and evaluation.

In recent years, there has been a perceptible shift from 'library as a storehouse model' to 'library as a gateway model'. Echoing similar views, Dougherty and Hughes[2] say that the concept of virtual library, i.e., a library that provides access to electronic and print materials from many sources, both local and remote, has achieved a widespread popularity, while Michalko[3] stresses that the 'research library must move with minimal disruption from a library model directed primarily at ownership of materials to one in which access and delivery play a central role'. A similar line of thinking can be seen in Dowlin[4] comment for 'the need to transform the library from a fortress to an information pipeline".

However, the current deviation indicates that in future the access would be preferred over the ownership in libraries. It is anticipated that materials in electronic form would be more popular than text and the cost of using would determine the policy of accessibility over ownership. However, browsing and serendipity would be adversely affected by the access mode despite the availability of browsing. The reason is that scanning access is not a satisfactory alternative to scanning printed pages. Also in case of monographs and books routine online access is not yet available.

Lancaster[5] has identified the following problems of electronic resources associated with access in collection development, i.e., integration of electronic resource with traditional forms; costs of Acquisition vs Access; and critical problem of determining what collection development really means in electronic environment. The other policy implications pertaining to collection development vis-à-vis electronic resources are the absence of bibliographic control, difficulty in identification and review; absence of proper selection tools; absence of a developed system for publication and distribution of electronic resources etc. As a matter of fact it identifies other problems and issues relating to the collection development aspect that are the cost ;finding out what is available; evaluating the sources available; and acquiring and servicing the sources required.

Stoller[6] comments on a prospective problem; i.e., dealing with electronic journals and suggests three options such as either print the journal directly from the only source or by down loading and manipulating through word processing software; to download the online file to an electronic medium, and provide access through PCs; and to maintain the file on a mainframe computer and provide access through LAN.

While deciding between ownership and access in relation to periodicals and monographs, Line[7] believes that remote access to both is inferior to on-the-spot access (ownership). Even in the case of local availability, studies in USA and UK indicate that though 70% of material wanted by researchers is held in the library, but only 60% of the items held are available when they are wanted. Also, while choosing between the alternatives of buying and borrowing, the deciding factor allowed should not be cost alone as exposure and browsing are vital criteria as well. Also due to the following two reasons, cost comparisons are not possible.

i. Cost of access is not stable;

ii. Before deciding as to whether resource materials should be owned or accessed, future use has to be anticipated which is a challenging task. However, the task is made easy by passing on the cost of access to the users but it might lead to a precarious situation where libraries rely mainly on accessing and buying nothing. In the on going debate different alternatives have been suggested, like acquisition or lease of CD-ROMs (ADONIS) of full or acquisition of tailor-made CD-ROMs. Other possibilities are synopsis journals, mini print and tabloid publications.

Analyzing the pros and cons of both ownership and access mode, it is advised to redefine the collection development policy which ensures on-the-spot access (through ownership) to material and remote access to older material. In addition, it should also encompass strategies to be adopted for selection and acquisition of resources in print, electronic and other formats.

While reframing the collection development policy statement another aspect that requires due consideration relates to weeding and stock regulation which is expected to enhance the services to readers for weeding and the concerned alternatives need to be carefully outlined. The collection development policy document should also entail methods pertaining to evaluation for traditional and electronic volumes.

The issue relating to cooperation and remote access are also vital aspects of the collection development policy. This in effect, suggests the planning for a resource sharing mechanism among participating libraries which would facilitate collective as well as remote access to the entire clientele.

The procedure relating to the selection and acquisition of materials in order to establish an expanding collection and also for decisions relating to the various materials to be included in the collection fall under the purview of Collection Development Methods. The inclusion of methods of selection and acquisition for traditional as well as conventional printed material is common but the evolving concept is of the use of electronic facilities (including networks) for collection development activities.

Use of Networks for CD-related activities that are receiving patron requirements for new books, journals and media; requesting and providing Inter Library Loan (ILL) to other libraries; requesting and providing missing issues, duplicates and exchange; requesting and ordering library materials; identifying document sources; getting quick copyright mission; communicating with vendors and customers; accessing electronic journals and newsletters however include subscribing to electronic publications; searching remote catalogues and union lists; searching online systems; scanning journals' tables of contents; retrieving files via FTP; receiving documents and technical data and searching files for acquisition lists and articles.[8]

A comprehensive treatment is needed on the main uses of networks for collection development. The advent of internet has revolutionized the entire spectrum of activities constituting, library management, be it collection management, be it information services management, be it document delivery services (electronic), and so on. There are certain crucial issues that require to be duly addressed in a network environment, including copyright management, standardization, training and education as these would facilitate effective utilization of valuable resources and power tools available on networks.[9]

Though Resource Sharing (RS) has a long and traditional existence, it has recently become an area of great interest to librarians and IT professionals and also a likely direction for future development. Libraries should think "material as community resources rather than with a simple institutional orientation", "local ownership to collective access".[10] etc. Also, for labeling organization arrangements in order to achieve a variety of resource sharing objectives, an array of terms such as consortium, network and cooperative have been used. Resource Sharing activities have been growing at a rapid pace all over the world and have been adequately supported by developments in IT and its widespread availability in support of networking. However, Resource Sharing as an operational concept has not gained sufficient ground in India.

Perhaps, it is time that information professionals should realize that provision of access to information is more important than collection building. There is an urgent need to strike a balance between local ownership and network access which should be reflected in the collection development policy statement. Consequently, librarians must shift the focus of their acquisition policy from the collection of materials an individual library to policies that weigh the merit of acquiring the same resources by consortia of local libraries, regional library cooperatives and state library networks.[11]

However, where electronic sources are concerned, they should not be acquired if it is possible to remotely access them. Their selection activity is slightly different from the selection of other material and the librarians have to look for alternatives to satisfy an existing demand and they need not have to purchase in anticipation of future demands.

The importance and usefulness of networks and networking can be gauged from Chaudhry's statement(s)[12]:

"Network' information resources, as extension of library collections and as bibliographic and communication utilities with their unprecedented connectivity, speed of transmission, and worldwide breadth have created excellent opportunities for libraries. Networks provide navigational tools and associated services which can be used by libraries to access remote resources for browsing, searching, and even downloading. They are redefining the concept of collection and collection development and transforming the selection, preservation, communication, and liaison functions in libraries. They are creating a powerful new context for the theory and practice of collection management and requiring librarians to develop new skills, accept new responsibilities, and change their ways of performing various library operations."

In case of network, Internet is a relevant example which facilitates selection and procurement of information material, document delivery, and provides access to electronic journals and other specialized material for acquiring, processing and accessioning information electronically. The three basic applications of internet are e-mail, remote login and file transfer.

The concept of collection evaluation can be viewed and analyzed under both macro and micro terms. In case of former the focus is on entire collection while in case of the later it is on a document or journal. From another point of view it can be said that there are primarily three aspects in collection evaluation — ownership, availability and accessibility. All the three aspects apply to the traditional collections but ownership in particular is not relevant to electronic sources. The main purpose, however is to ensure that the collection satisfies the users in a cost-effective manner. Obviously, there is the need for performance measures. In case of a traditional library, the size and variety of its collections were the main measures of excellence. Other measures used include exhaustiveness and quality, availability of documents, their brows ability, circulation and reference use, document exposure i.e. hours of use of a book by the reader, etc. Performance evaluation of collection can be determined through questionnaires surveys, interviewing, observation, library statistics, and other collection-centred and client-centred methods.

But, in the context of electronic resources, client-centred methods can be used keeping in view the two dimensions of evaluation—of availability and accessibility. In case, they do not exist, they would have to be developed. On the other hand, in evaluating traditional library collections, a host of evaluation methods have been developed in recent times viz., checklist approach, comparative holdings statistics, availability studies, standards, formulas, etc. Irrespective of the method used for the purpose of collection evaluation, it would be ensured that its main object is satisfied as a result satisfying the needs of users. Some of the collection management performance indicators useful in this context are relevance, delivery, effectiveness (use and satisfaction), cheapness, cost-efficiency and staff efficiency.

Information Technology can be used in libraries and information centre as a leverage to achieve excellence in the field of research and education, for the creation of knowledge society in the 21st century, where knowledge plays a role of primary production resource instead of capital and labour. Use of technology advancement in library and information centre has metamorphically converted the traditional repositories of knowledge into powerhouses of knowledge that are able to create, distribute and access information resources through computer networks.

At this juncture, it may be useful to remember that four interrelated trends of IT viz., multiple IT, dispersing IT, accelerating IT, and pervasive IT — can alter, the following:

- Objectives and strategies—the nature of sources and services
- Operational Structures – the ways in which service are delivered. In addition, the advantages of IT including accommodation of increased workload, achievement of greater efficiency, ability for generation of new services, facilitating cooperation, etc., can stand in good stead in the quest for quality and productivity of library and information sources collection and services.
- Development in information technology has not only

changed the way information is generated, organized, stored and distributed but more importantly have become indispensable to learning and research. In order to keep pace it becomes indispensable for learning and research. Keeping pace with advancement of IT and to meet the changing need of the academicians, it is imperative on the part of library professional to acquire the new skills required so as to provide wide range of library services especially in the culture of IT and ITES.

One of the questions for which an answer should be sought is: What does the future hold for collection development in libraries and information handling institutions? At this juncture, it would be appropriate to recall the functions that relate to collection development and its management specifically its selection, acquisition, archiving and preservation, policy making, collection evaluation, etc.

The spectrum of collection management is expanding and it is extending beyond the traditional concept of acquiring material, formulation of policies on housing, preservation, storage, weeding, discarding stocks, etc.

Economic constraints are very often adversely affecting funds related to acquisition and maintenance of books and associated facilities. Infact the prices of books and the subscription rates of serials are rising faster than the inflation rate.

The current scenario where there are new areas of concern in higher education viz.'information explosion' and growth of new information media. It has led to a situation where there is greatest need for effective and planned collection. The tremendous growth and importance of information technology is very significant. Despite its negative effects, in today's world one cannot service without information technology because of its persuasive nature. It only has to be closely monitored to ensure its effectiveness.

The falling costs dramatically have significant impact

on library operations. The impact is especially, on information resource development and information services. The challenge we face to-day is not a 'paper less society' nor the 'electronic information centre' but to maintain, nurture and optimize the resources of the libraries with the help of new technology.

The Impact of Information Technology on library operations is evident and undisputed. IT is related to all aspects of library operations viz., collection development policy, selection and acquisition of information materials, resource sharing and networking, collection evaluation, etc.

In this changing scenario, libraries and librarians will continue to play an important role in handling traditional as well as conventional and electronic resources. Unless this role is recognized, there is every likelihood that other professions and professionals will usurp their own roles and functions. The change in the operating environment and advantages of IT has to be realized and incorporated in the day to day library activities. However, one should be realistic and not be totally dependent on the new technologies. It should be borne in mind that they are only tools of our trade. We should not be too much enthusiastic and in awe of it. Also, it need to be examined whether, the existing collection development and management activities is complementary with the new technologies. If it is possible to integrate it should be done. In case there is a problem, some changes in the design and operation of the existing system would be required. In other words, a reappraisal of the existing system vis-à-vis new technology should be undertaken.

A similar line of thinking can be seen in the statement of Margaret Johnson[13] who says "libraries in their central role as providers and organizers of information cannot afford to ignore computer files or to approach them in a piecemeal fashion' or Alberico's comment that if we don't become involved at all levels, there is a very real possibility that resources will shift to other segments of the economy that can (handle and) deliver the electronic services that academic and post-industrial organizations will need to survive .Summer

Hill's observation that clearly groups of local users will have an ongoing need for the proximate location of heavily used data. In a dynamic networked environment the main objective of the library acquisition process should be to integrate the local collections of heavily used electronic resources and the provision of network access to less frequently used resources."

According to Atkinson[14], the role of the library in an IT-based environment would be: (a) To identify resources that are likely to be of greatest interest locally and downloading these to a local database—a kind of deferred collection development operation (locating information sources as they are needed rather than to predict the needs in advance) ;(b) Uploading should be preferred over downloading for being an efficient publisher and disseminator of information.

Holding a similar view Alberico comments that libraries may become publishers by using the network to build customized multi-media documents for clients or by providing the technology/training, and facilities to allow clients to build their own composite documents. Hence, the role of library is enhanced and it is viewed as information provider and for facilitating user education which also implies value-added responsibilities on user education.

On the role of librarian, Chaudhary[15] comments that librarians will have to initiate the transition to an access-based model of service based upon electronic networks that will provide bibliographic, numeric, and full-text information to scholars and researchers. They will have to create an environment where access to collective scholarly resources supercedes the historic quest for the great comprehensive collections. Among other significant roles is that of gatekeeper whose main function is helping to identify that part of information resources among the collection which is most vital to a particular user or group of uses. Shreeves[16] believes that clearly gatekeepers of this type will still be needed in the future, and perhaps, will be even more important than they are today. Also, librarians will have to expand their functions and also be a part of the process of access and negotiation with publishers and vendors about site licenses and methods of royalty and copyright payments. They would have to develop an insight and vision in order to be professional in selecting and acquiring material in the dynamic and complex environment.

Planning should be an essential parameter for collection development in libraries and should be given due consideration. It is easy to identify the various disciplines in which courses are conduced, but sharing the available funds among various departments of study and research is a tricky task. It should be ensured that distribution is done judiciously and allotment of funds to various disciplines is done on the basis of need. The same policy should be followed in case of peripheral subjects as well as for developing new disciplines, special funds collection should be created for the purpose.

Books pertaining to academic disciplines should be based on the recommendation of subject committees or departmental councils constituting the teachers of the respective academic departments. Separate funds should be allotted for books of general nature which interest or serve the needs of the teachers. Selection of books of this nature should be done by the university librarian or a senior most library staff who have a sound academic background and general knowledge. The quality of books should be ascertained so that they confirm to a certain academic standards.

Magrill and Gorbin[17] have proposed a new allocation plan for university libraries. According to this 25% of the material budget should be directed towards general reference material, special collection and other purchases that can not be directly related to specific academic programs. Another 25% should be assigned to a section which deals with the purchase of material for individual academic departments and are needed for instruction and research in a single department. The remaining 50 percent of the budget would be allocated to eight disciplinary clusters which comprise of academic units having common research interest and needs for library materials. The amount of the allocation given to each disciplinary cluster and each individual department would be based on factors commonly used in budget allocation formulas, such as: number of student credit hours generated; number of student credit hours by academic level; number of full time faculty by the department; average cost per book by the department, and average cost per periodical by the department.

The process of book acquisition should be a continuous one. Once the budget has been allocated at the beginning of the year, there is a need for formulation of a policy and guidelines relating to the procurement of books. For this purpose a meeting of the Heads of the departments or their representatives is required to be arranged effectively in order to streamline the procedure.

It is usually seen that university campuses are located at the outskirts of the city or in remote villages where there are no public libraries. Therefore, there is also a demand for books for general reading. However, the issue of acquiring books for promoting leisure reading is still a debatable question. Most of the campus libraries do acquire such materials, but it is not very desirable. The main reason behind is the belief that the purpose of procuring popular fiction would promote and encourage non-serious readers and there would be frequent re-binding needs and also the possibility of selecting cheap fiction. Maintaining quality standards would also be a daunting task.

Generally a special grant is made by the University Grants Commission when a new course or a research project on a new topic is started, with the purpose of purchasing essential books and thus developing the basic collection. Collection development on special topics such as area studies may be the result of local needs and environment for which scattered books in different shelves are grouped within as a special collection. For the continuous development of this collection, it should be ensured that a fraction of the funds is set aside for the purpose.

Users' surveys can be taken up by the different schools

of library science for the purpose of evaluating the collections and the findings of such studies should be implemented in the best possible manner. In addition to this an inbuilt mechanism should also be developed in libraries for assessing users' requirements. Cooperation of faculty members and newly enrolled members should be sought in this regard. A cooperative mechanism should also exist where staff members provide the readers with all essential services. In this connection, it is imperative to make a note of the areas which require improvement and forward the same to the concerned.

Menou[18]advocated certain standard collection development policies such as (i) the objectives to be achieved should be clearly set out in the form of goals to be acquired;(ii)Resources are specified for achieving goals;(iii)Delegation of responsibilities for goal completion; and (iv)Compilation of rules and policies to guide and regulate the implementation of the methods.

There is an urgent need to develop proper collection for the university libraries pertaining to central university libraries of UP, in order to satisfy the needs of the fundamental processes of higher education (predegree, post -degree, research, training of staff and the university extension) on the basis of a greater cooperation between the libraries. There is also a focused need to establish a collection with updated bibliographic material including authors of repute. For the purpose of the collection development and for acquiring information, best approaches are recommended. An environment should be created which must encourage cooperation in the process of collection, acquisition and maintenance between the university libraries. In order to enrich, maintain and strengthen, the bibliographic heritage of universities, a subject-wise quality collection be developed and maintained. It is also to ensure that obsolete items are timely discarded. There is an urgent need for establishing an affective policy and programme.

The different university libraries should be held responsible for the establishment of the collection development policy of the cooperation system as a whole. Each one of the librarians should be entrusted with the control. The policy should be of universal nature and must be adopted by all the university libraries of the Centres of Higher Education.

The selection of documents would preferably be in English. Documents in each Hindi, Urdu and other regional languages should also be included.

Giving due importance to the basic bibliography and research in each case, selection and acquisition of documents should be in line with the subject fields of study in the university and the lines of research of the centres. Amongst the available material, an effort should be made to select and acquire the best.

Acquisition of resources in the electronic format and digitization of printed documents should also be organized. The monographs and serial publications should be acquired in printed format as well.

For selection of necessary information resources, the order to be used is preferably the standard bibliographic sources and also the internet and specialized subject databases. For selection of information, one must carry out bibliometric studies in order to know the authors and their publications which are most important in a subject. It is also essential to obtain a list of the basic and complementary bibliographies. A process should be initiated which would entail the procedure to institute, the consultation of librarians with the heads of the university courses and researchers. There should be a mechanism to select sources in consonance with the study plans and the areas of research is the process of acquisition of the sources already selected one of the fundamental steps for achievement of the objectives in the collection development policy. It involves (a) Cooperative purchase will be specifically treated, by all The universities and centers of research with similar profiles of careers and fields of study will associate in the form of small consortia in order to acquire the necessary information;

and(b) To maintain the collection of exchange and gifts as complementary in order to acquire necessary information.

Keeping in view the dynamic growth of resources in a university library, there are certain parts of the collection which are not used and discarding them is essential to maintain the quality of the collection. Hence, it is vital to establish parameters for weeding and de-selection of material in order to maintain the balance of the collection. Therefore, the university libraries and other research centers ought to carry out the certain policies; such as

i. At least once in every five years general discarding of the obsolete and no longer uses material must be carried out.

ii. According to the criteria and advice of the subject specialists, systematic discarding be carried out by subject wise or group wise.

iii. Librarian of the particular library should be entrusted with the responsibility of discarding.

iv. Representatives of each area of the library such as services, processing and reference and heads of university departments and also the person in change of collection development should be made to participate in the process of discarding.

v. The physical state of documents, and their use the by users of system, updateness of subjects and the quantity of examples by title around be borne in mind to ease the physical availability of the collection.

vi. The primary and secondary collection and their index of growth, circulation, use and other factors should be systematically considered for evaluation.

vii. Discarded or weeded out documents should be offered as gifts and on exchange to other university libraries that respond to the subject in which discarded documents are available. If certain respondents do not reply in a stipulated time, material should be offered to other users.

NATIONAL KNOWLEDGE COMMISSION AND ROLE OF THE UNIVERSITY LIBRARIES

Education is pivotal to augment strong bond in human capital base which per se functions as pedestal in skill building and national innovation systems. This entails a holistic approach to education development. An encyclopedic programme of lifelong learning and education encompassing early childhood development, primary, secondary, tertiary and adult education needs to be brought under the rubric of overall development framework of each country. This shall sanguinely be instrumental in engineering the Millennium Development Goals (MDGs) by 2015.

Taking cognizance of the state of affairs, the Planning Commission of India in 2001 picked off a task force to carve out a set of strategies for transferring India as knowledge superpower. In sync with it, National Knowledge Commission (NKC) was instituted. The NKC brought to fore that education in any of its manifestations — primary, secondary, higher is of paramount significance. Inter-alia, higher education has made sizeable in roads to multifarious rungs of economic development, social progress and political democracy in independent India.

Under the rubric of expansion, NKC has given four most significant recommendations. Firstly the higher education system entails a huge expansion of opportunities to around 1500 universities nation wide that would enable India to garner a gross enrolment ratio of at least 15 percent by 2015. Revamping the system of regulation for higher education is also entailed. The Commission has suggested augmenting the public spending and diversifying the source of financing. Further the commission has recommenced the setting up of 50 National Universities.

Under the caption "Excellence" the National Knowledge Commission (NKC) has brought out those existing universities must restructure the undergraduate colleges and thus promote enhanced quality.

While bringing to force the powers of higher education, the NKC has also acknowledged and re-echoed public libraries as cardinal ingredient of the foundation of knowledge economy. NKC has brought out that there is far reaching unanimity for ushering sea-sized reforms in Libraries and Information Services (LIS) sector. NKC has recommended the following for designing strategies in the LIS sector.

Firstly, there is an urgency for setting up a permanent, independent and financially automoneous National Commission on Libraries as a statutory body to cater to all the information and learning needs of the citizens of India. Further, a national census of all libraries should be brought out by making a nation-wide survey.

NKC has taken earnest note of current education, training and research facilities. Correspondingly the NKC has suggested the mission or a commission to take the stock of manpower requirements of the country in the area of LIS management and take pertinent and relevant initiatives to meet the country's requirements through LIS education and training.

It is also urgently required to gauge the manpower requirements for different types of libraries and the teaching departments of library and information science. Further, it is quite urgent to constitute a central library fund for updating the existing libraries over a span of 3 to 5 years. It is urgently required to modernize library management and initiatives should be taken to optimize the potent of different types of libraries through new collaboration.

The degree of community participation in library management needs to be intensified and different stakeholders and user groups should deliberate in managerial decision-making process of libraries.

Information Communication Technology (ICT) application needs to be ushered in all libraries. Along with it, a National Repository of Bibliographic Records entailed to be instituted.

India has huge private and personal collections which must be spotted, registered and preserred for future. A model must be brought out for spotting out personal collection. The organizations should be educated in order to safeguard donations of personal collection through a simple way.

In the globalized era, the mechanism of Public-Private Partnership has garnered substantial currency in every sphere. The Public-Private Partnership (PPP) should be invoked to bring up new libraries.

Libraries are centers of disseminating information where involvement of IT is crucial as it profoundly affects both the organizational structure as well as the purpose and service of the library. Hence, libraries and librarians have little choice but to attune and adopt IT for library operations, especially for collection development activities and information services. Despite its enormous potential, information technology—be it optical disc technology or be it computers and communications technology —is not utilized to its full potential by libraries and information centres. Therefore, it is necessary that information professionals examine and design appropriate strategies in the selection and use of emerging technologies in order to enhance the productivity in library operations like collection development and management, and improving the quality of services to the users.

In this process of re-appraisal, it would be helpful to try the six R's of selecting new technologies—namely, review the mandate or mission of the library or information centre; refocus the direction to keep in step with the clients and the information environment; redefine your client's needs; relate with the staff and suppliers who are the providers of external information; revamp the activities and services; and recreate by using the tools of the future, i.e., new technology.

While analyzing collection development and its management one should bear in mind that the primary issues would revolve around; ownership vs. access, cooperative efforts, and evaluation. Ownership implies building up of collections and the significance of this activity would never subside as printed material would always be an integral constituent part of the collection. But, the growing importance of networked and local electronic resources are an interesting prospect, libraries require a mix of both ownership and access. The issue left therefore must be addressed is to decide as to what to own and what to access for older material and ownership for current material leading to the concepts of 'core access' and 'core collection'. This appears appropriate as the increase in acquisition yield diminishing returns. By implication, it would mean the need for a policy for weeding and stock relegation would lead to leaner, fitter libraries, which is the need of the hour. It is therefore, implied it implies that libraries need to shed the unnecessary fat of unused old stock and not to lose the muscle that current material gives. This is necessary as otherwise 'it would lead to the danger of combining bulimia (accumulating as much old material as they can lay hands on) with anorexia (starvation of current proteins and vitamins). Hence, it can be safe to assume that the cost of access would not fall in future. Thus, achieving a balance between local collections of heavily used traditional and electronic resources and the provision of network accessed documents should be the goal of the library acquisition process in an electronic networked information environment. However, the provision for the establishment of document delivery should be done in the beginning only.

On the other hand, to keep the information professionals updated with the knowledge and the skills required for handling information technology, course modules need to be designed both for formal as well as continuing education programs. As this would ensure the involvement and role of librarians and information scientists in establishing relationship between information resources and people in the future information oriented society.

At this juncture, it would be appropriate to quote Foskett who remarks 'At such a historic moment when new technology offers librarians and information officers the chance to make a real contribution to enhancing the cultural heritage by active exploitations of all its records, it would be a tragic irony if the medium becomes the message, technology becomes the master and not the servant and librarians find themselves once more cast in the role of keepers, not of books, but of machines. Librarians must not neglect their role as repositories, but become also mediators and promoters of communication'. The librarians must be ready to assume new responsibilities and roles and be gatekeepers and prospectors doing the job of acquiring material sources in an environment where networking is a critical element. The librarian infact should strive to become a creator, publisher and disseminator of information and also to have some value-added responsibilities on user education.

To conclude, the challenge we face is neither a 'paperless society' nor the 'electronic information centre'. The challenge is to maintain, nurture and optimize the resources of the libraries with the help of new technology. Thus the librarians must be in a frame of mind where they can accept technology emotionally, professionally and financially.

A collection development in a university library is a complex job and requires careful insight and analysis to clearly and defines the purpose. Therefore, it is imperative to formulate policies and programs by a committee or a group of faculty members representing various faculties. It is also necessary to involve the entire staff for developing a balanced collection.

Collection development is a vital and complex subject and its importance and significance is expected to increase by many leaps and bounds in future for the purpose of organization of information. It is essential to establish and maintain the quality and services of the collection for which the process of selection and acquiring of information sources need to be carefully monitored. Hence, collection development process requires the setting up of an efficient and updated policy framework to govern and lay down procedures and proceedings that aid the job of the professional managers involved and facilitate the decision making by them. The information policies have to be dynamic in order to adapt to the changing requirements of the organization and provide information to its members.

REFERENCES

1. Slamecka, V. (1985), "Empirical Issues in National Information System Design", paper presented at the International Symposium on Computerized Information Retrieval, Beijing, pp. 15-39.
2. Dougherty, R. M. and Hughes, (1991), *Preferred Futures for Libraries*, Research Libraries Group. Mountain View, California
3. Michalko, Quoted in Seetharama, S. (1997), "Collection Development/Management in an Information Technology Based Environment : Current Initiatives and Issues", *DESIDOC Bulletin of Information Technology*, Vol. 17 No. 1, p. 13.
4. Dowlin, K. E., "The Neographic Library", *In Libraries and Future.*
5. Lancaster, F. W., *Collection Development in the year 2025.*
6. Stoller, M. E. (1992), "Electronic Journals in the Humanities : A Survey and Critique", *Library Trends*, Vol. 40, pp. 647-666.
7. Line, M.B. (1996), "Access Vs Ownership : How Real an Alternative Is" *IFLA Journal*, Vol. 22, pp. 35-41.
8. Seetharama, S. (1997), "Collection Development/ Management in an Information Technology Based Environment : Current Initiatives and Issues", *DESIDOC Bulletin of Information Technology*, Vol. 17 No. 1, pp. 11-20.
9. Chaudhry, A. S. (1996), "Exploiting Network Information Resources for Collection Development in Libraries", *IFLA Journal*, Vol. 22, pp. 191-198.

10. Seetharama, S. (1997), Op.cit. p. 16.

11. Summerhil, C. A. "Quoted in Lancaster, F. W., *Collection Development in the year 2025.*

12. Choudhary, A. S. (1996), "Op.cit, pp. 191-198.

13. Johnson, M. (1990), "Adding Computer Files to the Research Library : Issues in Collection Management and Development", in Constance, C (Ed.), *Computer Files and the Research Library*, Research Libraries Group, Mountain View, California.

14. Atkinson, R. (1990), "Text Mutability and Collection Administration", *Library Acquisitions : Practice and Theory*, Vol. 14, p. 356.

15. Chaudhry, A. S. (1996), Opcit.

16. Shreeves, E. (1992), "Between the Visionaries and the Luddites : Collection Development and Electronic Resources in the Humanities", *Library Trends*, Vol. 40, p. 579.

17. Margrill and Garbin (1989), *Acquisitions Management and Collection Development in Libraries*, 2nd ed., ALA, p. 58

18. Menou, M. (1990), "Information Policy and National Development : An Educational Perspective", paper presented at the seminar FID/ET, Havana, p. 14.

Appendices

APPENDIX A

GUIDELINES FOR A COLLECTION DEVELOPMENT POLICY USING THE CONSPECTUS MODEL

International Federation of Library Associations and Institutions Section on Acquisition and Collection Development 2001

Foreword

This booklet is a brief guide on how to write a collection development policy, making use of the Conspectus methodology. It is the result of the recognition by the IFLA Acquisition and Collection Development Section that its worldwide members lacked a handy introduction to this important subject. The guide is intended to be of particular value to staff new to collection development and in areas where there is little written tradition of collection development. We hope that it will be of practical use to librarians setting out on the sometimes daunting task of writing a collection development policy.

The booklet was written by Dora Biblarz with the assistance of other members of the A&CDStanding Committee: Marie-Joelle Tarin, Jim Vickery and Trix Bakker. The text is also available, in both English and French, on the IFLA website at http://www.ifla.org/VII/s14.

Standing Committee of the IFLA Acquisition and Collection Development Section

March 2001

Contents

GUIDELINES for a COLLECTION DEVELOPMENT POLICY, using the CONSPECTUS model

Why A Written Collection Development Policy?

The library's primary task is to select, maintain, and provide access to relevant and representative information resources. Due to technological developments, libraries are, in the main, moving from holdings ('just in case') to access ('just in time') strategies. This implies that collecting policies are significantly changing and that libraries need to disseminate widely information on their collecting policies. A policy statement is a kind of framework and set of parameters within which staff and users work. It serves many functions beyond being merely a tool for selection of materials. In addition to describing current collections, it forces the staff involved to (re)consider the aims and objectives of the organization, both long and short term, and the priorities to be attached to different activities. It assists with budgeting, serves as communication channel within a library and between the library and outside constituents, supports cooperative collection development, prevents censorship, and assists in overall collection management activities, including the handling of gifts, deselection of materials and serial cancellations.

The main reasons for having a written collection development policy can be put under four broad headings:

1. Selection

The primary function of a written collection development policy is to provide guidance to staff when selecting and deselecting (printed and electronic) resources for the local collection. The document serves as a guideline for each stage of materials handling. It might cover the selection, acquisition, processing, housing, weeding, retention, preservation (archiving in case of electronic resources), relegation and discard of all types of library material in the relevant subjects, with reference to specified levels of collection depth and breadth. This reduces personal bias by setting individual selection decisions in the context of the aims of collection building practice, and identifies gaps in collection development responsibilities. It ensures continuity and consistency in selection and revision. Moreover, it clarifies the purpose and scope of local collections, and allows selection decisions to be evaluated by, for example, identifying what proportion of in-scope published material has been acquired. Such a reference guide reduces the need of selectors to raise recurrent questions, and assists in the training of new staff. It also provides useful information to other library staff whose work is collection based.

2. Planning

A policy document provides a sound foundation for future planning, thereby assisting in determining priorities, especially when financial resources are limited. This provides a basis for the fair allocation of resources, and helps to protect library funds by explaining the rationale behind acquisitions bids. Having a formal publication to refer to ensures continuity and avoids confusion. Compilation of a formal document is beneficial in itself, in that it involves acquiring knowledge of existing collection strengths, and obliges staff to reflect on the library's goals. The stated aims help other collection-related activities such as cataloguing, preservation and storage to form a coherent strategy, and support reader services, for example by identifying areas that are ripe for deselection, or more suitable for inter-library loan, document delivery or Internet access than for acquisition.

3. Public relations

Formal policy statements can be useful in making the case for the library when dealing with both its users, administrators and funding bodies. They support the stated objectives of the organization, demonstrating accountability and commitment to agreed goals. Ideally, the compilation of the document requires the active participation of both users and administrators, thereby improving communication between the library and its clientele. The policy statement serves as a contract with the library's users; it has the function to demonstrate to individuals within an institution what they can expect of the library both in form of collections and of services. It enables individual selection decisions to be justified on a standardized basis. By referring to the official statement, library staff can deflect criticism or censorship arising from special interest groups, and politely but firmly refuse unwanted gifts, sectarian materials or potentially offensive items.

4. The wider context

As individual libraries are increasingly unable to provide all their services by themselves, they are banding together into cooperatives, alliances and consortia. For these ventures to work, there must be mutual knowledge and agreement on which library is collecting what. A written collection development policy therefore often serves as a basis for wider cooperation and resource sharing, whether in a locality, region, country, or even internationally.

COLLECTION DEVELOPMENT POLICY ELEMENTS

A. Introduction

The main reason to write a collection development policy is to prevent the library from being driven by events or by individual enthusiasms and from purchasing a random set of resources, which may not support the mission of the library. Besides, electronic resources are becoming increasingly important to libraries of all types and sizes, and are consuming an ever-increasing share of library budgets. Therefore, selection decisions concerning electronic information resources should also be made within an explicit collection development policy. This might be separate policy or an integrated one.

The first elements of a collection development policy will be a mission statement of the library, the purpose of this policy and the audience to whom it is addressed. It should also include brief statements about the community or user group(s); description of the types of programs the library collection serves; the size (including number of periodicals, monographic volumes, electronic resources, languages represented) of the collection; a detailed budgetary overview of the money the library will spend on the different types of information resources; and any formal or informal cooperative agreements that affect the collection policy or practices.

B. General Statements

Here will be listed characteristics that determine the direction of the development of the collection such as: current focus only or also retrospective acquisitions; the resource types (monographs, periodicals, theses, gray literature, maps, etc.); languages; formats (printed, non-print or electronic); special sources of funding (a grant or gift from a donor); the policy regarding gifts and any special policies regarding maintenance (weeding, discarding, preservation) of the collection; and size of the collections. Other statements can be about how complaints are handled; if there is an equivalent to the "Library Bill of Rights"; about other relevant policies; what limitations exist - what subjects or areas are intentionally not collected etc.

C. Narrative Statements

Each institution, including its community and other constituents, is unique. Therefore, its policy statements will be unique. The policy statements should reflect this particular library and the community it serves.

- Statements should be made of special subject or format collections that represent unique materials and for which special guidelines apply, and which formats are excluded.
- The scope of coverage should be described (languages collected or excluded; geographical areas covered and/or specific areas excluded; chronological periods covered by the collection in terms of intellectual content and in terms of publication dates and specific periods excluded).
- Subjects should be described in terms of the library's classification scheme and subject descriptors.
- Library unit or selector responsible for the collection(s).
- Other categories of useful local information, such as interdisciplinary relationships; consortial relationships; policies for acquiring access to information.

- Other factors of local importance.

D. Subject Profiles

This section of the policy is based upon collection assessment (also referred to as collection evaluation) and needs periodic updating to reflect progress towards goals or goal revision due to changing circumstances. The preferred presentation is a set of conspectus reports, which include all appropriate collection information. Conspectus means an overview or summary of collection strength and collecting intensities – arranged by subject, classification scheme, or combination of either, and containing standardized codes for collection or collecting levels and languages of materials collected. Such a conspectus is a synopsis of a library's collection or of a consortium's or network's coordinated collection development overview or policy. The first conspectus was developed by the Research Libraries Group (RLG) and was subsequently adapted by other groups such as the WLN (Western Library Network). The information should be provided for each conspectus division (24), category (500) and subject (4000) evaluated by the library. See the Appendix for the list of the 24 Conspectus Divisions.

The assessment is achieved by a number of steps which include planning, gathering data, assigning collection depth indicators (or levels) and language codes. This information is used to manage the library's resources and to make other decisions relevant to the general operations.

E. Collection evaluation methods

The techniques and processes used to gather data for collection assessment are briefly described below. The data ideally describe in a succinct fashion the strength and depth of existing collections and provide a basis on which to assign collection levels.

Some techniques are essential and should be used consistently, while others are valuable under certain circumstances and not always necessary. It is up to the individual conducting the evaluation to select the methods, which will be used for each segment of the collection. This decision is based upon the availability of data, the amount of staff and other support available, and the goal for the final outcome (hcw it will be used in the library/institution). The techniques available for evaluating collections may be divided into two groups: those that are primarily collection-centered and those that are client-centered. Collection-centered techniques examine the content and characteristics of the information resources in order to determine the size, age, scope and depth of the collection in comparison to an external standard. Client-centered techniques describe how the collection is used and indicate the effectiveness of the collection relative to use. Collection assessment is likely to be most accurate and produce the most useful results when combinations of client-centered and collection-centered techniques, including both quantitative and qualitative results are employed in the data gathering and description process.

Quantitative Measures

Quantitative measures reveal size, age, use, costs and other numeric data. Examples of quantitative measures include inventory, or shelf list measures to determine actual title or volume counts, by segment or subject area. Median age or similar measures indicate the currency of the materials. Amount expended for acquisitions in a segment or subject area per year illustrates the ongoing commitment to develop that area. Percentage of titles owned by a library when compared to a standard list shows the breadth and depth of the collection. Use statistics (including internal library use and ILL) are both collection and client-centered.

Qualitative Measures

Qualitative measures are obtained through subjective evaluation and involve the professional judgment of librarians, appraisal from subject experts, or the opinion of customers. These techniques include impressions of the condition, character and appropriateness of a section of the collection. Another qualitative technique is the judgment made by comparison of one subject in the collection to a similar subject in another library, or to a subject bibliography.

F. Collection depth indicators

The collection depth indicators, or levels, are numerical values used to describe a library's collecting activity and goals. Three aspects of collection management are considered: current collection level, acquisition commitment, and collection goal.

Collection depth indicator definitions (see Appendix 2):

0 = out of scope

1 = minimal information level

2 = basic information level

3 = study or instructional support level

4 = research level

5 = comprehensive level

G. Language codes (RLG)

E: English language material predominates; little or no foreign language material is in the collection.

F: Selected foreign language material included in addition to the English material.

W: Wide selection of material in all applicable languages. No programmatic decision is made to restrict materials according to language.

Y: Material is primarily in one foreign language. The overall focus is on collecting material in the vernacular of the area.

H. Language codes (WLN)

P: Primary language of the country predominates — little or no other language material

S: Selected other language material included in addition to the primary language

W: Wide selection of languages represented

X: Material is mainly in one language other than the primary language of the library and country

I. Policy implementation and revision timetables

This describes the process for implementation, timetable for revision and other official adoption issues and introduces the notion of control.

Control

- Check the regular and pertinent application of the collection development policy on future acquisitions
- Call into question standing orders and subscriptions; thus apply retrospectively current policy standards on existing collections and relegate documents not fulfilling updated objectives.

Revision

- Re-examine the policy text at a frequency to be determined in order to detect insufficiencies and integrate new needs or recent modifications such as budget cuts, new curricula, etc.

APPENDIX 1 : WLN/OCLC CONSPECTUS DIVISIONS

Division	*Prefix LC*	*Prefix Dewey*
AGRICULTURE	AGR	AGD
ANTHROPOLOGY	ANT	AND
ART & ARCHITECTURE	ART	ARD
BIOLOGICAL SCIENCES	BIO	BID
BUSINESS & ECONOMICS	ECO	BUD
CHEMISTRY	CHE C	HD

COMPUTER SCIENCE	COM	CSD
EDUCATION	EDU	EDD
ENGINEERING & TECHNOLOGY	TEC	END
GEOGRAPHY & EARTH SCIENCE	GEO	GED
HISTORY & AUXILIARY SCIENCES	HIS	HID
LANGUAGE, LINGUISTICS & LITERATURE	LLL	LAD
LAW	LAW	DLA
LIBRARY SCIENCE	LIS	DLS
MATHEMATICS	MAT	MAD
MEDICINE	MED	DME
MUSIC	MUS	MUD
PERFORMING ARTS	PER	PED
PHILOSOPHY & RELIGION	PAR	PHD
PHYSICAL EDUCATION & RECREATION	PHR	DPH
PHYSICAL SCIENCES	PHY	PUD
POLITICAL SCIENCE	POL	POD
PSYCHOLOGY	PSY	PSD
SOCIOLOGY	SOC	SOD

APPENDIX 2 : CONSPECTUS COLLECTION DEPTH INDICATOR DEFINITIONS

The following revised Conspectus collection depth indicator definitions were developed in 1996and early 1997 under the auspices of the Association of Research Libraries with the help of WLN (Western Library Network). More than 30 active Conspectus users from the United States and abroad worked together to update the original language in a way that would improve the use of the definitions without diminishing the value of assessments that had employed the original definitions.

The revised definitions are the result of a conscious attempt to make them uniformly applicable to all subjects. Consequently, the definitions are generic. Supplemental guidelines have been and should continue to be developed to communicate common sets of understanding about the definitions within the context of a particular subject or area, e.g., fiction, children's literature, architecture, etc.

The revised definitions also reflect the need to deal more adequately with non-print and electronic forms of information and access/ownership issues in collection development.

For topics requiring information in non-print formats at the Basic Information level and beyond, it is assumed that appropriate visual, aural and other materials will also be collected, e.g., dance music, etc. To determine the appropriate collecting levels for topics in which non-print resources are essential, add the phrase "appropriate non-print media" to the line detailing the collecting of monographs and reference works. For example, Basic Information Level for a music collection would include "a limited collection of monographs, reference works and appropriate non-print media materials."

Relevant electronic resources are equivalent to print materials at any level as long as the policies and procedures for their use permit at least an equivalent information-gathering experience. Electronic journals, whether remotely or locally stored, are equivalent to print journals if

1. access to the electronic resources is at least equal to the print product;
2. there is access to a sufficient number of terminals; and
3. the information comes at no additional cost to the patron.

Similarly, a full text electronic archive of monographs, periodicals, images, etc., whether loaded locally or accessed over the Internet, is also equal to the original format if patron access and cost are equal or superior.

Document delivery services that are not instantaneous are not the same as those providing immediate availability on-site or electronically. The Conspectus measures resources owned by a library and its branches, if any, or those resources that are immediately accessible. The Conspectus does not measure what is obtained on a delayed basis from another library system or vendor, whether the delay is 10 hours or 10 days. Nonetheless, Conspectus users should feel free to provide details in the Notes Field about library user services which supplement but do not replace the library's owned resources.

CONSPECTUS COLLECTION DEPTH INDICATOR DEFINITIONS

0 Out of Scope.

Library does not intentionally collect materials in any format for this subject.

1 Minimal Information Level

Collections that support minimal inquiries about this subject and include:

- A very limited collection of general materials, including monographs and reference works.
- Periodicals directly dealing with this topic and in-depth electronic information resources are not collected.

The collection should be frequently and systematically reviewed for currency of Information. Superseded editions and titles containing outdated information should be withdrawn. Classic or standard retrospective materials may be retained.

2. Basic Information Level

Collections that serve to introduce and define a subject, to indicate the varieties of information available elsewhere, and to support the needs of general library users through the first two years of college instruction include:

- A limited collection of monographs and reference works.
- A limited collection of representative general periodicals.
- Defined access1 to a limited collection of owned or remotely-accessed electronic bibliographic tools, texts, data sets, journals, etc.

The collection should be frequently and systematically reviewed for currency of information. Superseded editions and titles containing outdated information should be withdrawn. Classic or standard retrospective materials may be retained.

3. Study or Instructional Support Level

Collections that provide information about a subject in a systematic way, but at a level of less than research intensity, and support the needs of general library users through college and beginning graduate instruction include:

- An extensive collection of general monographs and reference works and selected specialized monographs and reference works.
- An extensive collection of general periodicals and a representative collection of specialized periodicals.
- Limited collections of appropriate foreign language materials, e.g. foreign language learning materials for

non-native speakers or foreign language materials about a topic such as German history in German.

- Extensive collections of the works of well-known authors and selections from the works of lesser-known authors.

Defined access to an extensive collection of owned or remotely-accessed electronic resources, including bibliographic tools, texts, data sets, journals, etc.

The collection should be systematically reviewed for currency of information and for assurance that essential and important information is retained, including significant numbers of classic retrospective materials.

4. Research Level

A collection that contains the major published source materials required for doctoral study and independent research includes:

- A very extensive collection of general and specialized monographs and reference works.
- A very extensive collection of general and specialized periodicals.
- Extensive collections of appropriate foreign language materials.
- Extensive collections of the works of well-known authors as well as lesser-known authors.
- Defined access to a very extensive collection of owned or remotely accessed electronic resources, including bibliographic tools, texts, data sets, journals, etc.

Older material that is retained and systematically preserved to serve the needs of historical research

5. Comprehensive Level

A collection in a specifically defined field of knowledge that strives to be exhaustive, as far as is reasonably possible (i.e., a "special collection"), in all applicable languages includes:

- Exhaustive collections of published materials.
- Very extensive manuscript collections.
- Very extensive collections in all other pertinent formats.
- A comprehensive level collection may serve as a national or international resource.

BIBLIOGRAPHY

Anderson, Joanne S. (Ed.). Guide for written collection policy statements, 2nd ed., Chicago IL.: American Library Association, 1996. (Collection Management and Development Guide, 7)

Atkinson, Ross. "The language of the levels: reflections on the communication of collection development policy." College and Research Libraries, 47 (1986) 2, pp. 140-149.

Bakker, Trix. "Collectieprofielen in bibliotheken." In: Handboek informatiewetenschap voorbibliotheek en archief, onder red. van G.M. van Trier, D.W.K. Jansen, H. Prins, Alphen aanden Rijn: Samsom, 1996-....Oktober 1998b. IV D 200, pp. 1-21.

Biblarz, Dora. "The Conspectus as a blueprint for creating collection development policy statements." In: Collection Assessment: A Look at the RLG Conspectus. New York: Haworth Press, 1992, pp. 169-176.

Billings, H. "Library collections and distance information: new models of collection development for the 21st century." Journal of Library Administration, 24 (1996) 1/2, pp. 3-17.

Bushing, M., B. Davis and N. Powell. Using the Conspectus method. A Collection Assessment handbook. Lacey, WA: WLN, 1997.10

Calenge, Bertrand. Les politiques d'acquisitions. Paris: Editions du Cercle de la librairie, 1994.(Collections bibliothèques ; ISSN 0184-0886)

Calenge, Bertrand. Conduire une politique documentaire. Paris: Editions du cercle de la librairie, 1999. (Collections bibliothèques ; ISSN 0184-0886)

Cassell, K. Ann and Elisabeth Futas. "Collection development policies." Collection Building, 11(1991) 2, pp. 26-29.

Dowd, Sheila T. "Formulation of a collection development policy statement." In: Collection Development in Libraries: a Treatise. Greenwich, Conn.: JAI, 1980, pp. 67-81 (Foundationsof Librarianship, vol.10A).

Evans, Robert W. "Collection development policy statements: the documentation process."Collection Management, 7 (1985) 1, pp. 63-73.

Farrell, David. "Policy and planning." In: Collection Management: A New Treatise. Greenwich,Conn.: JAI, 1991, pp. 51-65.

Frank, D.G. et al. "The relevance of collection development policies: definition, necessity, and applications." RQ, 33 (1993) 1, pp. 65-74.

Futas, E. Collection Development Policies and Procedures, 3rd ed. Phoenix, Ariz.: Oryx, 1995.

Gaudet, Françoise et Lieber Catherine. Désherber en bibliothèque: un manuel pratique derévision des collections. Paris: Editions du Cercle de la librairie, 1996

Gestion, la, des collections: dossier. Bulletin d'informations de l'Association des bibliothécairesfrançais, n°166, 1995.

Hazen, D.C. "Collection development policies in the information age." College & ResearchLibraries, 56 (1995) 1, pp. 29-31.

Intner, Sheila S. "The ostrich syndrome: why written collection development policies areimportant."

Technicalities, 16 (July/August 1996), pp.1-3.

Johnson, R. "Collections development policies: a cunning plan." Technicalities, 14 (1994) 6, pp.3-6.

Kachel, Debra E. "The written collection development policy." In: Collection Assessment and Management for School Libraries. Preparing for Cooperative Collection Development. Westport, Conn.: Greenwood, 1997, pp. 53-76.

Snow, R. "Wasted words: the written collection development policy and the academic library."Journal of Academic Librarianship, 22 (May 1996), pp.191-194.

Vogel, K.D. "Integrating electronic resources into collection development policies." Collection Management, 21 (1996) 2, p. 65-66.

White, Gary W. and Gregory A. Crawford. "Developing an electronic information resources collection development policy." Collection Building, 16 (1997) 2, pp. 53-57.

Wood, Richard J. and Frank Hoffmann. Library Collection Development Policies: A Reference and Writers' Handbook. Lanham, MD: Scarecrow, 1996.

ELECTRONIC RESOURCES

General

Acqweb's Directory of Collection Development Policies on the Web.

http://acqweb.library.vanderbilt.edu/acqweb/cd_policy.html

Collection development policies - French libraries on the Web

http://www.enssib.fr/autres-sites/poldoc/index.html

Collection development policies - selected

http://www.aber.ac.uk/~tplwww/e/cdp.html

Collection development policies – electronic

http://www.library.yale.edu/~okerson/ecd.html

Examples

Collection Development Policy / National Library of Australia

http://www.nla.gov.au/policy/colldevt.html

Collection Development Policy / Laval University

http://www.bibl.ulaval.ca/info/polsec.html

Information Resources Policy / University Library, University of Hertfordshire, UK.

http://www.herts.ac.uk/lis/services/inf_resources/inf_res_policy.html

Collection Development Policy for Internet Resources / University of Oregon Libraries, US,http://darkwing.uoregon.edu/~chadwelf/intesele.htm

Collection Development Policy for Offline Electronic Resources / University of Oregon Libraries,US:http://darkwing.uoregon.edu/~chadwelf/offlelec.htm

Collection Development Policy for Electronic Journals / University of Oregon Libraries, US:http://darkwing.uoregon.edu/~chadwelf/ejoupoli.htm

Collection Development Policies - Digital Libraries / Columbia University Libraries, US,http://www.columbia.edu/cu/libraries/about/colldev/digital-library.htm

Collection Development Policy / Arts & Humanities Data Service

http://ahds.ac.uk/bkgd/cppub.html

Collection Development Policy for Electronic Material / National Library of Canada

http://collection.nlc-bnc.ca/

Collection Development Policy for California Digital Library

http://www.cdlib.org/collections/

Collection Development Policy / National Art Library [UK]

http://www.nal.vam.ac.uk/pubs/nalcdp.html

Permission to reprint has been sought from IFLA

APPENDIX-B

Collection Development Policy

Louis J. Blume Library

St. Mary's University

Prepared: Summer 1989	by Margaret Sylvia, Assistant Director for Technical Services
Adopted: Summer 1989	by the Librarians of the Blume Library
Accepted: Fall 1989	by the Academic Council of St. Mary's University
Revised: Summer 2008	by Margaret Sylvia, Assistant Director for Technical Services
Accepted: Fall 2008	by the Librarians of the Blume Library

Collection Development Policy

INTRODUCTION

The primary function of the Blume Library is to meet the information resource and service needs of the total University population as they relate to the curriculum of the University. The mission of the University is stated in full in the University catalog and includes goals of teaching, scholarly research, and service to the community. Library resources and services support these goals.

LOUIS J. BLUME LIBRARY MISSION STATEMENT

The Mission Statement of the Blume Library of St. Mary's University is as follows:

As a Community of Faith

Within a Catholic institution, the Blume Library maintains collections of particular interest to its Marianist mission and endeavors to support and affirm the work of all members of the University community by providing resources which reflect different perspectives and which foster intellectual growth.

Committed to an Educational Venture

The Blume Library strives to provide an environment in which students and faculty encounter and integrate the many branches of human knowledge by providing access to information regardless of format or location. The Blume Library responds to the changing needs of its clientele and is committed to making available new resources and services that foster educational excellence and in teaching their use to the community.

Dedicated to Scholarship

The Blume Library provides orientation, instructional programs, workshops, and written materials to assist students and faculty in their scholarly endeavors and participates directly in scholarship through research, publications, presentations, and workshop attendance.

Reaching Out in Service to Society

The Blume Library serves various communities in San Antonio, Texas, and North America through formal and informal sharing of resources and professional expertise.

Brief Description of the Community to be Served

The faculty, staff, and students of St. Mary's University are the primary community to be served. Students and faculty of the St. Mary's School of Law are the primary clientele of the Law Library and constitute a secondary clientele for the Blume Library. Clients of CORAL and TexShare members also constitute a secondary community for service. Finally, other members of the public will be served to the extent that this does not interfere with the primary mission of the library.

Specific Identification of Clientele

Faculty, staff, and students of the University will be served to the fullest degree possible through the use of instruction and reference help, however, the actual research will be done by the client. Reference librarians should strive to be proactive and seek out those clients who may need help. The collection will be developed according to the research and education needs of the students, faculty, and staff. Other patrons will be served to the extent that this does not interfere with service to the primary clientele. Service to TexShare members includes reciprocal borrowing privileges and rapid ILL through a special delivery service. At this time, due to budget constraints, the Blume Library cannot purchase materials in support of faculty research. Student study and research must be the primary focus of all library collection development. The library has, however, made arrangements with area colleges and universities for direct lending to faculty with appropriate University identification. If material needed does not exist in the San Antonio area, the library has access to the national pool of libraries participating in ILL through a relatively swift on-line lending system (OCLC). In the future, we hope to be able to support faculty research efforts directly. Library services to students at off-campus sites will be met through several means: online access for the library catalog and our information databases, delivery service for needed books, and faxing of journal articles to off-campus sites. A separate statement of library services to off-campus students is available.

Parameters of the Collection

Subject areas will be chosen to support the curriculum. Other materials, such as recreational materials, will be collected after curriculum needs have been met. Formats purchased include printed materials and, to the extent that these materials do not supply the needs of the curriculum, nonprint materials such as microforms, CDs, DVDs, and other needed formats, will be collected. Hardware to make appropriate use of the nonprint materials will be provided by the library. More specifics on the collection by subject area are noted below.

Needs to be Met

The collection is to be oriented toward educational purposes, at the general support level for the curriculum. Other appropriate purposes, such as recreation, may be represented at a minimum level. Most materials will be for circulation to the primary clientele except in special circumstances, e.g., reference materials, reserve materials, journals, and rare books and documents held in Special Collections.

Cooperation in Collection Development

The library will seek to cooperate with other libraries including cooperation in the areas of collection development, reciprocal borrowing, interlibrary loan, joint purchasing, shared cataloging, and any other possible areas of cooperation. However, as these programs are developed, the needs of the primary clientele should be considered. Cooperative programs should be planned to lead to enhanced service to the primary clientele. Since the funding for this library comes primarily from private sources, including a preponderate amount from tuition, we must be able to justify all cooperative programs in terms of increased service to the primary user.

Priorities of the Collection

Priority will be given to current educational materials in support of the curriculum at the basic and instructional/ support levels. Recreational and other materials may be collected to the extent that they contribute to a well-educated, well-rounded person. An explanation of the collection levels is given below.

The Blume Library collects materials on several levels.

Level one, the minimal level, is the level which attempts to build a highly selective collection in subject areas which, while they may not be represented in the curriculum, are appropriate in a library of an institution of higher education.

Level two is the basic level which supports lower level undergraduate study. It introduces and defines subjects offered at the 1000 and 2000 course levels. It includes works by major authors, basic works in the subject, and reference works. Subject dictionaries and encyclopedias, general surveys, and handbooks are types of materials collected at level two. Theatre and Art, two departments that do not offer a full major, are examples of departments at the level two collection level.

Level three, the instructional/support level, is designed to meet the instructional needs for an undergraduate major. It offers a wide range of general works, collections of works of more important writers, and provides support for specific courses at the 3000 and 4000 course level. Standard works, anthologies, major critical works and commentaries, classic works, and up-to-date general materials are types of materials collected at level three. Sociology, chemistry, and philosophy are departments at the level three collection level.

Level four, thesis level, supports research for theses

and dissertations. It covers major aspects of a discipline in greater depth and provides for instructional needs of students at this level. Types of materials collected at level four are graduate and professional-level current materials and retrospective materials in the field pertaining to degree programs. At this time, the budgetary resources of the library donot extend to providing full support for thesis research. Cooperation with other libraries is necessary for research at this level. Good examples of these departments include Counseling, English/Communications Studies and Political Science.

Standards for the Library and the Collection

Standards have been developed which provide a means of comparing individual facilities, staffs, and materials with recommended minimum and maximum levels of adequacy. Standards for College Libraries, Standards for Faculty Status for College and University Librarians, and Guidelines for Extended Campus Library Services have been approved by the Association of College and Research Libraries. Accreditation self-studies often ask for a general measure of the collection along with specific questions related to materials for the program being evaluated. These guidelines are also used for internal planning and evaluation.

CONSIDERATIONS IN COLLECTION DEVELOPMENT

Collection Evaluation and Maintenance

Systematic withdrawal of material no longer useful is essential in order to maintain a good library collection. Weeding criteria are generally the same as those used in selection. Physical condition, age of material, date of last loan, number of loans, number of copies in the collection, obsolescence of information, language of the material, existence and availability of indexes (particularly for periodicals and newspapers), coverage of the subject by other material in the collection, availability of the material from other libraries, listing of the item in important bibliographies, awards won, and other factors are relevant.Reshelving counts, citations in student and faculty bibliographies, and other factors may also be of use in weeding and collection evaluation decisions.

Periodical usage is evaluated on a continuing basis by counting the number of times each title is shelved. This is done on a limited basis for microforms as well. Periodical usage is not monitored during the summer when staffing is limited. Storage of low use periodicals will be kept at a minimum. In most cases, these titles will be offered for sale or for duplicate exchange.

Material selected for weeding may be placed in the storage area for a period of time prior to actual withdrawal. If the item is requested by a patron during the storage period, it should be returned to themselves. Worn or damaged materials which are still useful will be repaired or replaced if possible.

As specific areas of the collection are evaluated by librarian subject specialists, evaluation/selection plans should be prepared and submitted to the director of the library and the collection development department head for review. An evaluation/selection plan for a specific subject area should cover a number of points including a description of the courses being offered in the subject area and the names of the teaching faculty, the titles of bibliographic and selection aids to be used, any other collection evaluation aids to be used (citation counts, reshelving counts, circulation counts, etc.), the proposed budget for selection, what sort of approach to faculty will be made (memos, individual meetings, group meetings, etc.), proposed handling of weeded materials, and a tentative time-line for the evaluation.

Lost or Damaged Items

Library materials which have been lost or damaged will be replaced if they are still available in the current book trade, if they are considered appropriate for the collection (see Criteria for Selection), and as the budget allows. Clientele responsible are charged for the lost or damaged item plus a processing fee.

Gifts

Gifts may be added to the collection when they support the curriculum or add needed strength to the collection. Gifts will be accepted only when offered unconditionally to the library unless an exception to this policy is specifically made by the director.

Items added to the collection should be physically in good shape, i.e., no stains, mildew, missing pages, or writing in the item. The information should be current or classic. Gifts should generally meet the same criteria for selection as other new acquisitions. Magazines are not needed unless as replacements for missing issues in the collection or if a continuing gift is planned. The library does not evaluate gifts for tax purposes in accordance with IRS regulations.

Donors should be informed that the library, if unable to use the gifts, will dispose of them in an appropriate manner. Small gifts may be accepted by the director, acquisitions librarian or subject specialist. Larger collections should be examined by the library director, acquisitions librarian, and/or appropriate subject specialists before acceptance.

Library Instruction

Group instruction on the use of information resources is held on a regular basis in the library and one-on-one reference counseling is available from professional librarians. Librarians also act as contacts for departmental library instruction requests.

Circulation

Primary clientele of the library may check out material from the library for circulation. Number of items checked out at any given time and duration of the loan length is determined by the library. Fines are levied for overdue materials and replacement costs for lost or damaged materials will be collected. Interlibrary loan is available by request for primary clientele of the library.

Intellectual Freedom

The censorship policy of the library in brief notes that the official responsibility for selection resides in the Office of the President of the University but that this responsibility has been delegated to the Director of the Library. Since St. Mary's University is an institution of higher education no censorship can be tolerated. Materials are purchased in support of specific coursework and censorship would make much of that coursework impossible. Complaints in writing may be registered by primary clientele with the Director. The final decision on whether any item is placed in the library is not based on complaints but on the value of the item in meeting the research and educational needs of the primary clientele.

The library adheres to intellectual freedom standards as promulgated by the American Library Association and found in the appendices to this document.

Section 2.9.1.1 of the Faculty Handbook of St. Mary's University defines the parameters of academic freedom for librarians at the University. Academic freedom is accorded to all professional librarians because they are often present at the point of student contact with ideas. Librarians are free from fear of dismissal or reprisal for carrying out job-related tasks such as those listed below:

a. selection of publications, including determination of what to discard from an existing collection and what to accept or refuse from donors;

b. determination of restrictions on circulation or on access with regard to library materials;

c. determination of the degree of prominence in the shelving of selected library materials;

d. issuing of bibliographies that may include controversial publication; and

e. advising of students as to what to read or study.

Selection of Materials

Responsibility for Selection

Official responsibility for selection resides in the Office of the President of the University and actual responsibility has been delegated to the Director of the Library. The instructional faculty of the University has been given some responsibility for requesting selections in their fields. Professional librarians have the responsibility for selecting a core collection of materials using the subject allocations assigned to them and supplementing selections requested by the faculty. Beyond that, it is the responsibility of the acquisitions/collections development librarian to determine appropriate additions for the library's collection.

Budget

The Blume Library is responsible for developing a proposed budget according to the University-wide principles set forth each year. Customarily, the basis for this proposal is the previous budget with estimated adjustments to counteract the rate of inflation. In addition, any extraordinary support which may be needed for new courses and new curricula must be taken into account. The budget for materials is broken into separate budgets for serials, books, and other media. The books and serials budgets are further broken into allocations for particular subject areas on the basis of historical use and a specific allocations formula. Each librarian is responsible for selecting materials in one or more specific subject allocations and is encouraged to communicate with the instructional faculty in that area for collection development requests.

Selection Aids

Reviews and bibliographies may be used to aid selection with Choice being a primary selection tool, but absence of reviews need not bar selection of an item. Standing orders may be used to complete monographic series, however, these should be used with caution as costs increase. Vendors and jobbers both for monographs and serials may be required to bid for the library's business. The lowest bid will be selected unless experience has proven the bidder's service unacceptable.

The ACRL Standards for College Libraries indicates that the collection should contain a substantial portion of the titles listed in standard bibliographies for the curricular areas of the institution and for supporting general fields of knowledge. Subject lists for college libraries have been prepared by several learned associations, while general bibliographies such as Resources for College Libraries are especially useful for identifying important retrospective titles. A majority of the appropriate, current publications reviewed in scholarly journals and in reviewing media such as Choice or Library Journal should be acquired. Thus, librarians engaged in collection development should make extensive use of reviews and bibliographies as selection aids.

Criteria for Selection of Materials

a. Importance of the subject in relation to the curriculum

b. Currency and accuracy of information

c. Timeliness and importance of information

d. Author's reputation and significance

e. Availability of other material on the subject in the library, in other area libraries, and in print

f. Inclusion of the title in standard bibliographies or indexes

g. Recommendation in standard reviewing sources

h. Price

i. Length (prefer monographs 50 pages or more in length; monographs of less than 20 pages will not be added to the collection)

j. Language (English only is selected, except for those

items selected to support the foreign language curriculum)

k. Format, including legibility, binding, and type

l. Scope and depth of subject coverage

m. Ease of use

n. Publisher (vanity presses are normally excluded)

o. Duplication (single copies are normally collected unless there is an overriding need in the curriculum for duplicates of an item)

p. Current vs. retrospective materials (Both current and retrospective materials are essential to the needs of a University library, however, current materials will generally receive a higher priority. Current materials are those in-print in their original editions. Retrospective materials are those out-of-prints or available only as reprints either in full-size or microform editions.)

q. Out-of-print materials (Efforts to obtain materials from the out-of-print market will be made if it is judged that the material is of enough importance to justify these efforts and costs. Probability of use and frequency of use by primary clientele are factors in the judgment of importance.)

Selection of Special Formats

a. Paperbound vs. Hardbound Materials

Hardbound volumes are generally preferred for library use when both formats are available. However, if the material is judged to be of transitory usefulness and the cost of the paper volume is substantially less than the cost of the hardbound volume, the paper volume may be preferred. This is generally true if the paper volume is to be discarded through regular updating. If a quality paperback is available, it may be purchased and bound in lieu of purchasing a publisher-bound volume if the procedure is cost-effective.

b. Microform vs. Full-size Materials

Microform is a practical format for storage and retention of large collections of lesser-used materials. However, when possible, full-size materials will be purchased for ease of use.

c. Serials and Subscriptions

The Standards for College Libraries state that in general it is good practice to consider owning any title that is needed more than five times a year and recommends the use of Magazines for Libraries and other bibliographies. However, the Standards go on to state that it may not be necessary to subscribe to certain less frequently used titles if they are available at another library nearby, or if needed articles may be procured through a reliable delivery system or by electronic means.

Serials which present substantial information related to the curriculum and which are accessible through major abstracting and indexing services will be preferred for selection and retention purposes. Long runs of serials back files will rarely be purchased due to the generally higher priority given to current information needs, though short runs of back files (2-3 years) are generally useful. Subscriptions are purchased only with budgets secure for the long-term. Grants, gifts, and other short-term monies may be used for purchase of various library materials but subscription funds must be guaranteed for the future, including the possibility of increases for inflation. Due to the budgetary commitments entailed by subscriptions and standing orders, great care is needed in their selection. In order to have the widest possible coverage of periodical material, duplicate copies of subscriptions will generally not be purchased. As a general rule, the library will not purchase newsletter type material which may have a limited time span of usefulness.

The Periodicals Department of the Blume Library will evaluate each title for its timeliness. Online subscriptions when they match or exceed the content of print subscriptions are preferred. Some titles may be retained for a limited number of months or years. Titles received more frequently than monthly will in many cases be replaced by a microform or will be assigned a limited retention period. All titles which are permanently retained in the library and not replaced by microform will be bound.

d. Media

Media items, such as CDs and DVDs, will be purchased when print materials do not supply the needs of the curriculum. Hardware to make use of media collected by the library will be provided by the library. The media budget is too small to be allocated among the various academic subjects. Since that budget must be shared, the library has established the following priorities for the purchase of non-print media items:

The first priority for expenditures from the media budget will be to purchase those items which will be required for students to complete successfully a course being taught at St. Mary's University. The second priority for expenditures from the media budget will be to purchase those items that are recommended to students as an adjunct learning experience for a class being taught at St. Mary's University. If sufficient funds remain after February of the fiscal year, the library will seek to meet other media requests. The library will from time to time purchase additional media programs in the general interest of the University, but not required for classroom viewing.

Book and periodical budgets will not be used for the purchase of non-print media. Many academic departments have a great need for additional book funds. If a department has an excess of funds in its book allocation, these will be transferred to other departmental book allocations.

e. CD-ROM Indexes and Texts

CD-ROM titles received on deposit from the federal government will be added to the collection. CDROMs received as adjunct material with books will be added to the catalog and stored on the shelf with the book or other item they accompanied.

f. Audio Compact Disks

Audio CDs will be purchased by the library including classical, jazz, opera, and other musical genres as the budget allows. The library no longer collects musical recordings in other formats, such as LPs. Older formats may be weeded as they become unusable.

g. Electronic Information Access

Increasingly, materials are available electronically which are not accessible in any other format. These include electronic journals and books, online indexes, full text databases, and other information available through computer networks and other sources. Material in these formats is subject to the same scrutiny as other material added to the collection. Care should be taken in the collection of online full text material. Stability and accessibility of the resource will be a primary consideration. Cancelling paper or microfiche ownership of material in lieu of online access is sometimes, but not always, appropriate. The impact on the library's users must be considered if online access is terminated or diminished through contractual disputes or price increases.

Purchase of electronic books may be desirable under the following circumstances: there is an expectation of demand for the title, the purchase price is reasonable compared to paper, the title is purchased and not leased, and the online format is user-friendly. Electronic books should be cataloged and made available via links in the online catalog.

The library will provide access to these materials through collection and organization of such items as can be appropriately held in the library. In addition, the library will strive to provide its clients with online access to electronic sources of information as well as training and materials to aid them in searching for information online.

Specific Guidelines for Selection of Electronic Access Purchases for Books/Reference Materials

The following guidelines **must** be met for the purchase of online books and reference works. If these standards cannot be met, books and reference materials will not be purchased in electronic format.

1. Guaranteed ownership in perpetuity.
2. Low or no cost annual hosting fees
3. Availability of remote access via IP authentication
4. Availability of usage statistics, preferably COUNTER-compliant

The next sets of guidelines are preferred, but not absolutely necessary, for electronic purchases:

1. Ability to lend the material on Interlibrary Loan.
2. Administrative access to usage statistics at any time (not just "statistics by request")
3. Easy-use interface
4. Ability to download and read offline
5. Multiple simultaneous users
6. Prefer a purchase with guaranteed ownership that includes copy to be kept locally as a backup (on DVD or other appropriate format).

Collection Development Policy Review

The collection development policy will be reviewed (and amended if necessary) annually by the Acquisitions/ Collection Development Librarian in cooperation with the Director.

Special Collections Within the Library

Government Information

The Blume Library has been a selective depository of

government information since 1966. As such, it has an obligation to share federally provided documents with the general public. These materials may not be circulated outside the library except to St. Mary's students, faculty and staff, but are available at all times for use in the building and for request through ILL. New documents are fully cataloged and older uncataloged documents are being added to the catalog.

a. New Item Selection for Government Documents

New items made available for depository selection are scanned carefully and items are chosen based on several criteria:

1) Relevance of subject matter to St. Mary's curriculum or general needs; subject of topical interest; if the library has few books on a subject of general interest, series covering that subject is usually selected

2) Level of information presented (highly technical scientific items are not selected; items expected to contain only very elementary treatments are usually not selected)

3) Format and frequency of publications (single-sheet, pamphlet, poster and weekly publications are usually not selected unless the subject matter is of extremely high relevance)

4) Selection or likelihood of selection by Law Library and/or other depositories in the San Antonio area(regarding materials on the "borderline" between legal and other fields, especially in the case of major sets or series, the Law Library Documents Librarian should be consulted; in the case of major series inother subject areas, consult with all area reference librarians)

b. Some Specific Guidelines

1) Select all Census reports and explanatory publications, including reports for all states and regions are selected, in CD-ROM where possible (select an additional paper copy of Texas reports if possible).

2) For most other series broken down geographically, select only Texas reports or regional reports containing Texas information. (Exceptions: select all states if information is of substantial economic relevance; e.g., series from the Bureau of Labor Statistics).

3) Series featuring historical treatment of any subject are usually selected.

4) Subjects selected most comprehensively are: business, economics, psychology, labor, general statistics, foreign relations, drug abuse, criminal justice

5) Subjects selected most sparingly (or not at all) are: medicine, science (technical), engineering (technical), agriculture (non-economic)

c. Weeding Government Documents

Group 1: Weed frequently (every 2-3 years) of all eligible material (5 years or older) with very few exceptions.

Classes: A (except yearbooks, reference-type works, economic materials)

C 55

D (except historical and statistical publications)

E (except economic materials, documents concerning Texas)

EP (except economic materials, documents concerning Texas)

HE (medical sections)

P

TD

Y 4 (Committees selected in microfiche)

Group 2: Weed infrequently (every 5 years) of most eligible material (especially pamphlets, looseleaf items not updated, etc.) with frequent exceptions.

Classes: FEM (retain Flood Insurance Studies)

HH I (retain major series, reference books)

Y 4. En 2/3: (nominations, especially, can be weeded unless person is well-known or nomination was controversial)

Y 4.G 74/7, G 74/9: (nominations, especially, can be weeded unless person is well-known or nomination was controversial)

Y 4. Sci 2: (nominations, especially, can be weeded unless person is well-known or nomination was controversial)

Group 3: Do not weed (pamphlets, posters, unbound items and other publications which are "awkward" innature are weeded, but sparingly)

Classes: C (except as noted above)

GP

GS

HE (except as noted above)

J

L

LC (except: keep only 5 years of Monthly Checklist of State Documents)

PR

S

T

X

Y (except as noted above)

Manuscripts and Rare Books

Special Collections in the library consists mainly of materials dealing with Texas, the Spanish borderlands, and military history as well as 19th century mathematics. It also contains smaller collections of other materials. These documents are not yet cataloged.

Juvenile Literature

The juvenile literature collection is primarily composed of award-winning books, e.g., Caldecott and Newbery medal and honor books. Secondly, the collection contains books most often studied in children's literature classes. These items are fully cataloged. The following is a list of the types of books to be included in the St. Mary's Blume Library:

a. A basic reference collection related to the study of children's literature, including anthologies and books on the history of literature, authors, illustrators, teaching of literature, and storytelling. These will be included in the regular collection, many of them in reference.

b. Picture books, including wordless books, ABC and number books, with a well-rounded representation of various authors and illustrators.

c. Fiction for middle grade children (2rd-6th graders), jr. high readers, and young adults.

d. Folklore, including fairy tales, legends, stories to tell, and representative Southwestern folklore.

e. Poetry, including songs that may be used during practice lessons and student teaching.

f. Biography to the extent that it is studied in the children's literature courses.

g. Non-fiction to the same extent.

h. Spanish and bilingual books to support the trend toward multicultural education and to exemplify St.Mary's unique cultural environment.

Curriculum Collection

The textbook collection for use by the education students of St. Mary's is comprised primarily of the textbooks adopted for use in the state of Texas by the Texas Education

Agency. The library's goal is to have all the currently adopted textbooks for subjects taught at St. Mary's. Some older textbooks are retained to serve as a comparison to textbooks currently under adoption. These items are fully cataloged.

Leisure Reading

Fiction for recreational reading will be collected at a minimal level for those fiction items which do not directly support the curriculum. Recreational reading is located in the Leisure Reading area near the entrance to the library. Funds are used from such profit as may be realized from photocopying in the library. Genre fiction, such as romances, westerns, and so forth will not be collected specifically as a genre. Some genre fiction may be included in the minimal level collection of fiction. Best sellers will not be purchased solely because they are best sellers if they have no other purpose in the collection. Genre fiction, bestsellers, and other more popular items may be found in this collection. These items are fully cataloged.

Theses and Dissertations

Two copies of each St. Mary's University thesis or dissertation will be bound, cataloged and retained by the library. One copy will be kept permanently in Special Collections and one will be shelved in the regular book collection. Non-St. Mary's theses and dissertations which have been purchased by the library will be cataloged and added to the regular book collection.

Reserve Collection

The reserve collection is a collection of instructor-owned materials and materials owned by the Blume Library which have been separated from the larger collection for restricted use. A very few items belonging to the library which are expected to receive very high use and are in need of high security are placed on permanent reserve by the library. Most items in the reserve collection are placed on temporary reserve by instructional faculty.

Reference Collection

Great care should be taken in selecting materials to be placed in the reference collection since space is limited and circulation of these materials is restricted. Materials which may be placed in the reference collection include, but are not limited to: general and special encyclopedias or handbooks, periodical indexes, general and special dictionaries, directories, atlases, almanacs, and literary explicators. Books which might be expected to be read in full or receive infrequent use should be placed in the circulating collection. All books received in the Blume Library are examined by librarians before cataloging and agreement by two or more librarians is necessary for placement of the item in reference.

Reference Desk Collection

A ready reference collection is available for use at the reference desk. Since space in this area is extremely limited, only material which can reasonably be expected to receive heavy use by the reference librarians should be placed at the reference desk. These materials include, but are not limited to, titles such as Statistical Abstract, World Almanac, and the like. Agreement of two or more librarians is necessary for placement of an item at the reference desk.

Specific Subject Areas in the Collection

Please note that when specific items or titles are mentioned below, these are the minimum purchases that may be made. Other items should be purchased in addition to these if they meet collection development criteria and if the budget allows. These are Library of Congress classifications and may not correspond exactly to specific departments offering coursework at the University. The curriculum is constantly being updated and specific subjects which are mentioned are only indicative of the general direction of the curriculum, not as an exhaustive survey. Communication with teaching faculty on current and upcoming needs is essential.

A: General Works

Encyclopedias - At least one general encyclopedia should be available to the St. Mary's community online and one in print (for as long as print is an option). Specific subject area encyclopedias are purchased as needed.

Periodical Indexes - These will be provided in electronic format whenever possible at no cost to the user. Paper indexes supplement these services.

Dictionaries - An unabridged dictionary should be available and several good current desk-type dictionaries should be purchased each year or two for the reference collection.

Other necessary reference works should be purchased including general almanacs, handbooks, atlases, and more specific subject reference works, particularly those geared toward the curriculum. Statistics, almanacs and yearbooks should also be kept as current as possible but past years should be retained to verify trends. Older reference works should be considered for addition to the regular collection or storage.

This subject area should be developed reflecting the collection levels noted below.

B - BD: Philosophy

Older works can be valuable in this area so weeding should be selective. Philosophy by geographic area should be included, both Western and Eastern thought. Concentration should be given to areas of philosophy taught in the curriculum. These include history of philosophy both ancient and modern, ethics, philosophy of knowledge, philosophy of religion, social philosophy, American philosophy, logic and other topics. This subject area should be developed at collection level three.

BF - BJ: Psychology

General psychology texts and some popular topics may

be included such as intelligence, memory, and dreams. Concentration should be on the areas of psychology represented in the curriculum. Counseling needs should also be considered in collecting psychology books, particularly for upper level needs in this area. Many classic works exist in this area so weeding should be done carefully; however, tattered and obsolete works may be withdrawn.

Curriculum needs in psychology include topics such as tests and measurements, abnormal psychology, human sexuality, perception, physiological psychology, personality, social psychology, human development, industrial psychology, motivation, learning, experimental psychology, and human factors. Graduate study in clinical psychology and industrial/organizational psychology is also offered with similar topics covered in greater detail.

The counseling curriculum covers such topics as human relations, human services, substance abuse, family therapy, and group dynamics. Graduate work in counseling covers group processes, administration of counseling services, individual assessment, career planning, counseling ethics, mental health and psychopathology. As counseling is the first Ph.D. program offered by the University, collection development is particularly needed in this area to support the expanded curriculum and student research. This subject area should be developed at collection level four.

BL - BX: Religion

Religious texts of the major religions should be included, e.g., the Bible and the Koran. These items generally do not date quickly or at all so weeding may be selective, concentrating on very worn, damaged, duplicative or unused items. Comparative handbooks, encyclopedias, concordances, commentaries, dictionaries, histories, interpretations, sermons, church histories, church administration, and biographies on religious leaders should be available. This is an area that should be well developed with particular concentration on Christianity and the Catholic religion in keeping with the mission of the University.

The theology curriculum concentrates on theology from a Catholic perspective, Christian scriptures, the Christian community, marriage, justice, moral issues, ethics, sacraments, rites and symbols as well as personal religious transformation and topics in Marianist religious life. Graduate works in theology include score courses on biblical theology, systematic theology, Christian spirituality and religious education. This subject area should be developed at collection level four.

C - G: History and Geography

Biographies should be selected including reference works such as biographical dictionaries and collective biographies such as Who's Who in America at least. Biographies which support the curriculum, particularly in history, should be purchased. Historical material must be chosen carefully to represent a variety of viewpoints and should present history of all areas of the world. Current interpretations of historical events should be emphasized in the collection. Withdraw worn and unused items as necessary.

Reference works should include a good gazetteer, a chronology of history, and several atlases (historical, national, and international). Atlases should be replaced every five years or when appropriate to show major geographical changes. Travel books date quickly and should be replaced annually if possible. Current guides on the local area, the state, the U.S., Mexico, Canada, the national parks, camping in the U.S., the major European countries and Asia should be available at a minimum. Others may be purchased if the budget allows.

Curriculum topics in history include the history of the U.S. in overview and specifically regarding the Civil War, Texas and the South, world history both ancient and modern, and history of Latin America, Mexico, Spain, Germany, Russia and medieval and contemporary Europe. Graduate work in history covers similar topics but in greater detail and depth. This subject area should be developed at collection level four.

H: Social Sciences

Works on economics, business, and sociology should generally be less than 10 years old for educational purposes but many older works still have value for research purposes. Withdraw outdated and obsolete works throughout the social sciences. Generally, the social sciences should be developed at collection level four, however, each area is assigned a particular level.

HA: Statistics

Much of this material is available in federal, state, and local government documents. Census material and statistics on the city of San Antonio, Bexar County, Texas, the U.S. and the world as a whole should be included. Selected statistics on other areas and on specific topics may be collected as needed for the curriculum. Statistical material should be retained as long as possible since retrospective research on trends is common. This subject should be developed at collection level three.

HB - HJ: Economics

Books on economic theory and the various schools of economic thought should be included as well as abroad range of material on labor problems, money and banking, investments and finance. Writings of classic and contemporary economists should be covered. The free enterprise system and other methods of economic production should be included.

The curriculum includes topics such as principles of economics, monetary and fiscal policy, business and labor economics, urban economics, business cycles, and price theory. Graduate work in economics covers these topics as well as international relations and economics, regional income analysis, macroeconomics, microeconomics, wage and employment theories, welfare economics, econometrics, comparative economics and cost-benefit analysis. Consider unused items older than 10-15 years as candidates for weeding. This subject should be developed at collection level four.

HD: Business

Finance, investment, risk management, systems analysis, operations research, management information systems, and business statistics are covered in the business curriculum as well as general business, business policy, production management, human resources management, and topics in international business. Marketing principles, sales management, marketing research and other topics are also covered. Graduate study in business concentrates on many of these same topics as well as international business, multinational management and marketing and international banking. Current material on specific companies, managerial techniques and other covered topics should be selected. Consider unused items older than 10-15 years as candidates for weeding. This subject should be developed at collection level four.

HF: Accounting

General accounting, business law, fund accounting, auditing, personal and business income tax are covered in the curriculum. Many current items on tax law are available as government documents. Do not select workbooks. Do not duplicate material found in the Law Library. Unused material older than 10-15years should be examined for withdrawal. Select only very current material pertaining to the curriculum.

This subject should be developed at collection level three.

HM - HX: Sociology

Include specific items on women and on racial, ethnic and national groups. Marriage and family titles should be quite current, five years old or less. Weed carefully since these materials are frequently used by the Ph.D. students in the counseling program. Sociology of sex roles, religion, future societies, social issues, the family, minority relations, and death and dying are typical curriculum topics. Criminology, cultural anthropology, interviewing techniques, social issues and change, group dynamics, propaganda and public opinion, urban sociology, demography, and gerontology are also covered. Peace and justice are major themes. This subject area should be developed at collection level three. Marriage, family, and gender roles as topics should be developed at collection level four to support the counseling doctoral program in marriage and family therapy.

J: Political Science

Current and international viewpoints should be included to form a broad range of ideas. Types and forms of governments, suffrage, slavery and processes of government regulation should be covered by the collection. The curriculum focuses on federal, state and local government structures and functions, political parties, the presidency, legislation, political research, behavior and communication as well as jurisprudence, constitutional law, international law, and world politics including world security, foreign policy and politics in developing states and other countries. Graduate studies in political science focus on many of these same topics but in greater depth.

Public administration coursework is also supported by the political science collection and is designed as a professional program to prepare individuals for employment as administrators, planners, and managers at all governmental levels. Core courses include human resources policies, organizational behavior, research in applied economics, regional and urban economics, public administration, scope and methods of political science, and topics in public administration and urban affairs. Public administration is a graduate level program although an undergraduate minor is available. Unused material older than 10-15years may be considered for weeding. This subject area should be developed at collection level four.

JX: International Relations

International relations stress an interdisciplinary understanding of economics, history, and political science with a worldwide view. The curriculum promotes a broad knowledge of world events and international affairs. Graduate study in international relations concentrates on similar topics but in more detail and depth. Unused material older than 10-15 years may be considered for weeding. This subject area should be developed at collection level four.

K: Law

This area is well covered by the Law Library on campus so less coverage is necessary in the Blume Library. However, coverage of specific law enforcement issues should be purchased for the criminal justice and criminology curriculum. Criminology and criminal justice are interdisciplinary programs that draw on information from most of the social sciences. Covered topics in the curriculum include criminal investigation, legal aspects of law enforcement, criminal procedure and evidence, police-community relations, police administration, police role in crime and delinquency, world-wide public justice systems, and terrorism. Unused titles older than 10-15 years should be considered for withdrawal except for classic works on the law. This subject area should be developed at collection level four.

L: Education

General education, reading, educational psychology, educational administration (particularly of Catholic schools), and moral and religious education are emphasized. A basic collection of material on higher education should be included. Unused items older than 10-15 years should be considered for weeding. Under TEA guidelines, the library also collects juvenile literature and textbooks adopted by the Texas State School Board. Primary emphasis is on American public education, particularly in Texas, including new trends and developments, teaching methods and curriculum development. The education program specifically covers topics such as child and adolescent development, philosophy of education, classroom management, and the teaching of language, mathematics, social studies, science and reading. Physical education is also covered including topics on teaching in the elementary and secondary schools, and the coaching of football, volleyball, soccer, softball, and track and field as well as sports officiating, first aid, prevention of athletic injuries and analysis of human movement. This subject area should be developed at collection level four.

M: Music

Recorded music, librettos, and literature of music are included. Items do not date quickly and weeding may be very selective. A good music encyclopedia is essential. Choir, concert band, jazz laboratory, and brass, woodwind, percussion, vocal, piano, guitar and string ensembles are offered. Music literature, ethnic influences in American music, form and analysis, counterpoint, harmony, music history, arranging, conducting, and teaching of music at elementary and secondary levels are offered as well as marching band techniques and pastoral music. This subject area should be developed at collection level three.

N: Fine Arts

Visual arts, architecture, sculpture, painting, drawing, and other arts are covered. Items do not date quickly and weeding may be very selective. These tend to be expensive but also to have a long shelf life. Purchase the theoretical and classic materials as opposed to crafts and "how-to" books. Art history and artist biographies should be included. A good art encyclopedia is a necessity. Current reference works on movies, TV, radio, theater, and dance should be included. The art curriculum includes courses on drawing, design, painting, sculpture, print-making, art history, and teaching of art in elementary grades.

This subject area should be developed at collection level two.

P - PM: Language

Dictionaries for translating English into and from the foreign languages taught at St. Mary's as well as all other major languages are essential. Some self-teaching and beginning texts should be included. Other items may be included as required for the curriculum. Weeding in this area may be very selective since these items do not date quickly, however, worn and tattered items should be withdrawn in favor of newer materials.

French, German, Japanese, Latin, Spanish and Portuguese are offered in the curriculum; also offered is a concentration in studies in multinational organizations. French and Spanish literatures are covered in-depth. This subject area should be developed at collection level three.

PN: Drama

Introduction to the theater, voice and diction, acting, production, directing, rehearsal and performance, history of the theater, and creative drama for children are covered in the curriculum. Anthologies of plays for adults and children should be purchased as well as biographies of actors, directors, and producers. Classic as well as current plays should be purchased. Current material on acting, producing, and directing is needed. This material may be withdrawn when outdated but classic plays, anthologies, histories; and biographies may be retained unless worn. This subject should be developed at collection level three.

PN - PZ: Literature

Style manuals, quotation books, grammar and rhetoric handbooks, and general literature reference works such as Readers' Encyclopedia should be included. Purchase major authors and good anthologies by various type of literature as covered in the curriculum. Be in touch with the faculty for suggestions on what authors, titles, and subject areas they plan to teach in current and future semesters. These items should last, so weeding may be done selectively on badly worn items and tattered classic works should be replaced.

Reference materials should include works of summary and literary criticism as well as works on authors' biographies.

The curriculum concentrates on British, American, and Latin American literatures including Shakespeare, the British novel, the literature of American minority groups, and many other topics. Composition, creative writing, persuasive writing, and analysis of poetry, fiction and drama are also covered as well as journalism, technical writing, radio and television production, public speaking, oral interpretation, and persuasive speaking and debate. Graduate study concentrates on many of the same areas but in greater depth and detail. This subject area should be developed at collection level four.

QA: Mathematics

Algebra, trigonometry, calculus, probability, statistics, differential equations, discrete mathematical structures, complex variables, linear algebra, boundary value problems, geometry and numerical analysis are offered in the curriculum. Graduate study covers more complex mathematical problems such as linear statistical models, stochastic processes, analysis of variance and other statistical methods. Programmed texts on mathematical problem solving and biographies of important mathematicians should be purchased. Workbooks should not be selected. Weeding of unused and duplicative items should be considered. This subject area should be developed at collection level three.

QA 76: Computer Science

Programming in C++, Java and other languages are offered as well as an introduction to data structures, operating systems, computer systems architecture, compilers, database programming, software engineering, artificial intelligence, computer graphics, office automation and distributed data processing. Graduate study covers similar topics but at a more advanced level. Materials selected should be the most recent available. Unused materials more than 10 years old should be considered for withdrawal.

Selections should particularly include items covering software and hardware available for student use on campus. Consider both the computer center and personal computers available. The collection should include guides to personal computers and computing, handbooks on software and hardware, and a current dictionary and/or encyclopedia of computer science at a minimum. This subject area should be developed at collection level four.

QB - QC: Physics

Topics covered in the curriculum include mechanics, heat, acoustics, electricity, magnetism, optics, atomic physics, nuclear physics, thermodynamics, quantum mechanics and astronomy. Many classic works in physics exist which should be retained, however, currency of information is imperative. Unused materials older than 10-15 years should be examined for withdrawal. Purchase authoritative and general works as well as biographies of physicists and tables of physical values. Keep up with current topics such as superconductivity. This subject area should be developed at collection level three.

QD: Chemistry

General, organic, inorganic, analytical and physical chemistry are covered in the curriculum as well as chemical thermodynamics and biochemistry. Works on laboratory methods and tables of chemical values should be selected as well as other items in support of the curriculum. Unused materials older than 10-15years should be examined for withdrawal. This subject area should be developed at collection level three.

QE: Earth Sciences

General, physical and historical geology are covered in the curriculum as well as earth and energy resources, oceanography, meteorology, environmental geology, mineralogy, petrology, structural geology, geomorphology, paleontology, stratigraphy and x-ray analysis of crystalline materials. Materials purchased should be general with concentration on local and Texas geological features. Unused item solder than 10-15 years should be considered for withdrawal. This subject area should be developed at collection level two.

QH - QR: Biology

Food and nutrition, rcsearch methods, tissue culture, radiation biology, developmental biology, physiology, genetics, microbiology, immunology, medical microbiology, cellular physiology, molecular biology, and recombinant DNA techniques are covered in the curriculum. Unused works older than 10-15years should be considered for withdrawal. Some specialized dictionaries or encyclopedias are necessary as are anatomy and physiology guides with colored illustrations. Concentration is on a pre-medical type of curriculum. Biotechnology is a growing industry, particularly in San Antonio, and general works in this area should be purchased. This subject area should be developed at collection level three.

R: Medicine

There may be some overlap between the life sciences and medicine books. Collection development in this area should include a current medical dictionary, anatomy handbook, and standard drug handbook for reference work. Other items may be included to support the biology curriculum. Psychiatry texts should be purchased in support of the counseling curriculum. Medical ethics materials should also be collected. This subject should be developed at collection level three for general medical books and collection level four for psychiatry and counseling items to support the programs noted above.

S: Agriculture

This is a minimally collected area which does not directly support the curriculum; however, there is some overlap with biology as taught in the University, particularly in the area of nutrition. Dated, worn, and unused material may be weeded. This subject area should be developed at collection level one.

T: Technology

Engineering texts tend to be quite expensive and often become dated quickly. Avoid very specific topics in favor of more general works to support the curriculum. Unused works older than 10-15 years should be considered for withdrawal. Industrial and electrical engineering are accredited at the University and topics covered in the curriculum include engineering graphics, industrial statistics, work design, productivity measurement, engineering data processing, principles of materials science, engineering mechanics, simulation, quality control, production planning, industrial robotics, manufacturing systems, plant layout, operations research, strength of materials, and fluid mechanics, as well as electronics, electronic design, energy conversion, network analysis, switching theory, microprocessors, electromagnetics, semiconductor devices, analog filter design, control systems, and communication theory. Graduate work in industrial and electrical engineering includes most of these topics but approached from a more advanced level. This subject area should be developed at collection level four.

U: Military Science

ROTC students may receive a minor in Military Studies and the International Relations curriculum is also supported by this subject area. Dated, worn, and unused material may be weeded. This subject area should be developed at collection level two.

V: Naval Science

ROTC students may receive a minor in Military Studies and the International Relations curriculum is also supported by this subject area. Dated, worn, and unused material may be weeded. This subject area should be developed at collection level one.

Z: Library Science and Information Resources

Include LC Subject Headings, LC Classification Schedules, the Dewey Decimal Classification and Relative Index and any other current materials needed for the library. Bibliographies for use in specific subject areas are acquired as needed for collection development. Specific materials needed for library work should be purchased, however, collection level one is the aim for general coverage of library science. General information resources are also classified in this section and include such topics as information literature, online research skills, digital libraries, online ethics, online tools, etc., and should be developed at collection level two. Weeding of obsolete and unused material older than 10-15 years should be considered.

APPENDICES III : LIBRARY BILL OF RIGHTS

The American Library Association affirms that all libraries are forums for information and ideas, and that the following basic policies should guide their services.

I. Books and other library resources should be provided for the interest, information, and enlightenment of all people of the community the library serves. Materials should not be excluded because of the origin, background, or views of those contributing to their creation.

II. Libraries should provide materials and information presenting all points of view on current and historical issues. Materials should not be proscribed or removed because of partisan or doctrinal disapproval.

III. Libraries should challenge censorship in the fulfillment of their responsibility to provide information and enlightenment.

IV. Libraries should cooperate with all persons and groups concerned with resisting abridgment of free expression and free access to ideas.

V. A person's right to use a library should not be denied or abridged because of origin, age, background, or views.

VI. Libraries which make exhibit spaces and meeting rooms available to the public they serve should make such facilities available on an equitable basis, regardless of the beliefs or affiliations of individuals or groups requesting their use.

Adopted June 18, 1948.

Amended February 2, 1961, and January 23, 1980, inclusion of "age" reaffirmed January 23, 1996, by the ALA Council.

APPENDICES IV : INTELLECTUAL FREEDOM STATEMENT: AN INTERPRETATION OF THE LIBRARY BILL OF RIGHTS

The heritage of free men is ours

In the Bill of Rights to the United States Constitution, the founders of our nation proclaimed certain fundamental freedoms to be essential to our form of government. Primary among these is the freedom of expression, specifically the right to publish diverse opinions and the right to unrestricted access to those opinions. As citizens committed to the full and free use of all communications media and as professional persons responsible for making the content of those media accessible to all without prejudice, we, the undersigned, wish to assert the public interest in the preservation of freedom of expression.

Through continuing judicial interpretations of the First Amendment to the United States Constitution, freedom of expression has been guaranteed. Every American who aspires to the success of our experiment in democracy — who has faith in the political and social integrity of free men — must stand firm on those Constitutional guarantees of essential rights. Such Americans can be expected to fulfill the responsibilities implicit in those rights.

We, therefore, affirm these propositions:

1. We will make available to everyone who needs or desires them the widest possible diversity of views and modes of expression, including those which are strange, unorthodox or unpopular.

Creative thought is, by its nature, new. New ideas are always different and, to some people, distressing and even threatening. The creator of every new idea is likely to be regarded as unconventional, occasionally heretical, until his idea is first examined, then refined, then tested in its political, social or moral applications. The characteristic ability of our governmental system to adapt to necessary change is vastly strengthened by the option of the people to choose freely from among conflicting opinions. To stifle nonconformist ideas at their inception would be to end the democratic process. Only through continuous weighing and selection from among opposing views can free individuals obtain the strength needed for intelligent, constructive decisions and actions. In short, we need to understand not only what we believe, but why we believe as we do.

2. We need not endorse every idea contained in the materials we produce and make available.

We serve the educational process by disseminating the knowledge and wisdom required for the growth of the mind and the expansion of learning. For us to employ our own political, moral, or esthetic views as standards for determining what materials are published or circulated conflicts with the public interest. We cannot foster true education by imposing on others the structure and content of our own opinions. We must preserve and enhance the people's right to a broader range of ideas than those held by any librarian or publisher or church or government. We hold that it is wrong to limit any person to those ideas and that information another believes to be true, good, and proper.

3. We regard as irrelevant to the acceptance and distribution of any creative work the personal history or political affiliations of the author or others responsible for it or its publication.

A work of art must be judged solely on its own merits. Creativity cannot flourish if its appraisal and acceptance by the community is influenced by the political views or private lives of the artists or the creators. A society that allows blacklists to be compiled and used to silence writers and artists cannot exist as a free society.

4. With every available legal means, we will challenge laws or governmental action restricting or prohibiting the publication of certain materials or limiting free access to such materials.

Our society has no place for legislative efforts to coerce the taste of its members, to restrict adults to reading matter deemed suitable only for children, or to inhibit the efforts of creative persons in their attempts to achieve artistic perfection. When we prevent serious artists from dealing with truth as they see it, we stifle creative endeavor at its source. Those who direct and control the intellectual development of our children— parents, teachers, religious leaders, scientists, philosophers, statesman—must assume the responsibility for preparing young people to cope with life as it is and to face the diversity of experience to which they will be exposed as they mature. This is an affirmative responsibility that cannot be discharged easily, certainly not with the added burden of curtailing one's access to art, literature, and opinion. Tastes differ. Taste, like morality, cannot be controlled by government, for governmental action, devised to suit the demands of one group, thereby limits the freedom of all others.

5. We oppose labeling any work of literature or art, or any persons responsible for its creation, as subversive, dangerous, or otherwise undesirable.

Labeling attempts to predispose users of the various media of communication, and to ultimately close off a path to knowledge. Labeling rests on the assumption that persons exist who have a special wisdom, and who, therefore, can be permitted to determine what will have good and bad effects on other people. But freedom of expression rests on the premise of ideas vying in the open marketplace for acceptance, change, or rejection by individuals. Free men choose this path.

6. We as guardians of intellectual freedom oppose and will resist every encroachment upon that freedom by individuals or groups, private or official.

It is inevitable in the give and take of the democratic process that the political, moral and esthetic preferences of a person or group will conflict occasionally with those of others. A fundamental premise of our free society is that each citizen is privileged to decide those opinions to which he will adhere or which he will recommend to the members of a privately organized group or association. But no private group may usurp the law and impose its own political or moral concepts upon the general public. Freedom cannot be accorded only to selected groups for it is then transmuted into privilege and unwarranted license.

7. Both as citizens and professionals, we will strive by all legitimate means open to us to be relieved of the threat of personal, economic, and legal reprisals resulting from our support and defense of the principles of intellectual freedom.

Those who refuse to compromise their ideals in support of intellectual freedom have often suffered dismissals from employment, forced resignations, boycotts of products and establishments, and other invidious forms of punishment. We perceive the admirable, often lonely, refusal to succumb to threats of punitive action as the highest form of true professionalism: dedication to the cause of intellectual freedom and the preservation of vital human and civil liberties.

In our various capacities, we will actively resist incursions against the full exercise of our professional responsibility for creating and maintaining an intellectual environment which fosters unrestrained creative endeavor and true freedom of choice and access for all members of the community.

We state these propositions with conviction, not as easy generalizations. We advance a noble claim for the value of ideas, freely expressed, as embodied in books and other kinds of communications. We do this in our belief that a free intellectual climate fosters creative endeavors capable of enormous variety, beauty, and usefulness, and thus worthy of support and preservation. We recognize that application of these propositions may encourage the dissemination of ideas and forms of expression that will be frightening or abhorrent to some. We believe that what people read, view, and hear is a critically important issue. We recognize, too, that ideas can be dangerous. It may be, however, that they are effectually dangerous only when opposing ideas are suppressed. Freedom, in its many facets, is a precarious course. We espouse it heartily.

Adopted by the ALA Council, June 25, 1971.
Endorsed by the Freedom to Read Foundation, Board of Trustees, June 18, 1971.

APPENDICES V : THE FREEDOM TO READ

The freedom to read is essential to our democracy. It is continuously under attack. Private groups and public authorities in various parts of the country are working to remove or limit access to reading materials, to censor content in schools, to label "controversial" views, to distribute lists of "objectionable "books or authors, and to purge libraries. These actions apparently rise from a view that our national tradition of free expression is no longer valid; that censorship and suppression are needed to avoid the subversion of politics and the corruption of morals. We, as citizens devoted to reading and as librarians and publishers responsible for disseminating ideas, wish to assert the public interest in the preservation of the freedom to read.

Most attempts at suppression rest on a denial of the fundamental premise of democracy: that the ordinary citizen, by exercising critical judgment, will accept the good and reject the bad. The censors, public and private, assume that they should determine what is good and what is bad for their fellow citizens.

We trust Americans to recognize propaganda and misinformation, and to make their own decisions about what they read and believe. We do not believe they need the help of censors to assist them in this task. We do not believe they are prepared to sacrifice their heritage of a free press in order to be "protected" against what others think may be bad for them. We believe they still favor free enterprise in ideas and expression.

These efforts at suppression are related to a larger pattern of pressures being brought against education, the press, art and images, films, broadcast media, and the Internet. The problem is not only one of actual censorship. The shadow of fear cast by these pressures leads, we suspect, to an even larger voluntary curtailment of expression by those who seek to avoid controversy.

Such pressure toward conformity is perhaps natural to a time of accelerated change. And yet suppressions never more dangerous than in such a time of social tension. Freedom has given the United States the elasticity to endure strain. Freedom keeps open the path of novel and creative solutions, and enables change to come by choice. Every silencing of a heresy, every enforcement of an orthodoxy, diminishes the toughness and resilience of our society and leaves it the less able to deal with controversy and difference.

Now as always in our history, reading is among our greatest freedoms. The freedom to read and write is almost the only means for making generally available ideas or manners of expression that can initially command only a small audience. The written word is the natural medium for the new idea and the untried voice from which come the original contributions to social growth. It is essential to the extended discussion that serious thought requires, and to the accumulation of knowledge and ideas into organized collections.

We believe that free communication is essential to the preservation of a free society and a creative culture. We believe that these pressures toward conformity present the danger of limiting the range and variety of inquiry and expression on which our democracy and our culture depend. We believe that every American community must jealously guard the freedom to publish and to circulate, in order to preserve its own freedom to read. We believe that publishers and librarians have a profound responsibility to give validity to that freedom to read by making it possible for the readers to choose freely from a variety of offerings. The freedom to read is guaranteed by the Constitution. Those with faith in free people will stand firm on these constitutional guarantees of essential rights and will exercise the responsibilities that accompany these rights.

We therefore affirm these propositions:

1. *It is in the public interest for publishers and librarians to make available the widest diversity of views and expressions, including those that are unorthodox or unpopular with the majority.*

Creative thought is by definition new, and what is new is different. The bearer of every new thought is a rebel until that idea is refined and tested. Totalitarian systems attempt to maintain themselves in power by the ruthless suppression of any concept that challenges the established orthodoxy. The power of a democratic system to adapt to change is vastly strengthened by the freedom of its citizens to choose widely from among conflicting opinions offered freely to them. To stifle every nonconformist idea at birth would mark the end of the democratic process. Furthermore, only through the constant activity of weighing and selecting can the democratic mind attain the strength demanded by times like these. We need to know not only what we believe but why we believe it.

2. *Publishers, librarians, and booksellers do not need to endorse every idea or presentation they make available. It would conflict with the public interest for them to establish their own political, moral, or aesthetic views as a standard for determining what should be published or circulated.*

Publishers and librarians serve the educational process by helping to make available knowledge and ideas required for the growth of the mind and the increase of learning. They do not foster education by imposing as mentors the patterns of their own thought. The people should have the freedom to read and consider a broader range of ideas than those that may be held by any single librarian or publisher or government or church. It is wrong that what one can read should be confined to what another thinks proper.

3. *It is contrary to the public interest for publishers or librarians to bar access to writings on the basis of the personal history or political affiliations of the author.*

No art or literature can flourish if it is to be measured by the political views or private lives of its creators. No society of free people can flourish that draws up lists of writers to whom it will not listen, whatever they may have to say.

4. *There is no place in our society for efforts to coerce the taste of others, to confine adults to the reading matter*

deemed suitable for adolescents, or to inhibit the efforts of writers to achieve artistic expression.

To some, much of modern expression is shocking. But is not much of life itself shocking? We cut off literature at the source if we prevent writers from dealing with the stuff of life. Parents and teachers have a responsibility to prepare the young to meet the diversity of experiences in life to which they will be exposed, as they have a responsibility to help them learn to think critically for themselves. These are affirmative responsibilities, not to be discharged simply by preventing them from reading works for which they are not yet prepared. In these matters values differ, and values cannot be legislated; nor can machinery be devised that will suit the demands of one group without limiting the freedom of others.

5. *It is not in the public interest to force a reader to accept with any expression the prejudgment of a label characterizing it or its author as subversive or dangerous.*

The ideal of labeling presupposes the existence of individuals or groups with wisdom to determine by authority what is good or bad for the citizen. It presupposes that individuals must be directed in making up their minds about the ideas they examine. But Americans do not need others to do their thinking for them.

6. *It is the responsibility of publishers and librarians, as guardians of the people' s freedom to read, to contest encroachments upon that freedom by individuals or groups seeking to impose their own standards or tastes upon the community at large.*

It is inevitable in the give and take of the democratic process that the political, the moral, or the aesthetic concepts of an individual or group will occasionally collide with those of another individual or group. In a free society individuals are free to determine for themselves what they wish to read and each group is free to determine what it will recommend to its freely associated members. But no group has the right to take the law into its own hands, and to impose its own concept of politics or morality upon other members of a democratic society. Freedom is no freedom if it is accorded only to the accepted and the inoffensive.

7. *It is the responsibility of publishers and librarians to give full meaning to the freedom to read by providing books that enrich the quality and diversity of thought and expression. By the exercise of this affirmative responsibility, they can demonstrate that the answer to a "bad" book is a good one; the answer to a "bad" idea is a good one.*

The freedom to read is of little consequence when the reader cannot obtain matter fit for that reader's purpose. What is needed is not only the absence of restraint, but the positive provision of opportunity for the people to read the best that has been thought and said. Books are the major channel by which the intellectual inheritance is handed down, and the principal means of its testing and growth. The defense of the freedom to read requires of all publishers and librarians the utmost of their faculties, and deserves of all citizens the fullest of their support.

We state these propositions neither lightly nor as easy generalizations. We here stake out a lofty claim for the value of the written word. We do so because we believe that it is possessed of enormous variety and usefulness, worthy of cherishing and keeping free. We realize that the application of these propositions may mean the dissemination of ideas and manners of expression that are repugnant to many persons.

We do not state these propositions in the comfortable belief that what people read is unimportant. We believe rather that what people read is deeply important; that ideas can be dangerous; but that the suppression of ideas is fatal to a democratic society. Freedom itself is a dangerous way of life, but it is ours.

This statement was originally issued in May of 1953 by the Westchester Conference of the American Library

Association and the American Book Publishers Council, which in 1970 consolidated with the American Educational Publishers Institute to become the Association of American Publishers.

Adopted June 25, 1953; revised January 28, 1972, January 16, 1991, July 12, 2000, by the ALA Council and the AAP Freedom to Read Committee.

A Joint Statement by: American Library Association

Association of American Publishers

Subsequently Endorsed by:

American Association of University Professors

American Booksellers Foundation for Free Expression

American Society of Journalists and Authors

The American Society of Newspaper Editors

Anti-Defamation League of B'nai B'rith

Association of American University Presses

Center for Democracy & Technology

The Children's Book Council

The Electronic Frontier Foundation

Feminists for Free Expression

Freedom to Read Foundation

International Reading Association

The Media Institute

National Coalition Against Censorship

National PTA

Parents, Families and Friends of Lesbians and Gays

People for the American Way

Student Press Law Center

The Thomas Jefferson Center for the Protection of Free Expression

APPENDICES VI : FREEDOM TO VIEW STATEMENT

The Freedom to View, along with the freedom to speak, to hear, and to read, is protected by the First Amendment to the Constitution of the United States. In a free society, there is no place for censorship of any medium of expression. Therefore these principles are affirmed:

1. To provide the broadest access to film, video, and other audiovisual materials because they are a means for the communication of ideas. Liberty of circulation is essential to insure the constitutional guarantees of freedom of expression.
2. To protect the confidentiality of all individuals and institutions using film, video, and other audiovisual materials.
3. To provide film, video, and other audiovisual materials which represent a diversity of views and expression. Selection of a work does not constitute or imply agreement with or approval of the content.
4. To provide a diversity of viewpoints without the constraint of labeling or prejudging film, video, or other audiovisual materials on the basis of the moral, religious, or political beliefs of the producer or filmmaker or on the basis of controversial content.
5. To contest vigorously, by all lawful means, every encroachment upon the public's freedom to view.

This statement was originally drafted by the Freedom to View Committee of the American Film and Video

Association (formerly the Educational Film Library Association) and was adopted by the AFVA Board of

Directors in February 1979. This statement was updated and approved by the AFVA Board of Directors in1989.

Endorsed by the ALA Council January 10, 1990

APPENDICES VII : AMERICAN LIBRARY ASSOCIATION CODE OF ETHICS

As members of the American Library Association, we recognize the importance of codifying and making known to the profession and to the general public the ethical principles that guide the work of librarians, other professionals providing information services, library trustees and library staffs.

Ethical dilemmas occur when values are in conflict. The American Library Association Code of Ethics states the values to which we are committed, and embodies the ethical responsibilities of the profession in this changing information environment.

We significantly influence or control the selection, organization, preservation, and dissemination of information. In a political system grounded in an informed citizenry we are members of a profession explicitly committed to intellectual freedom and the freedom of access to information. We have a special obligation to ensure the free flow of information and ideas to present and future generations.

The principles of this Code are expressed in broad statements to guide ethical decision making. These statements provide a framework; they cannot and do not dictate conduct to cover particular situations.

I. We provide the highest level of service to all library users through appropriate and usefully organized resources; equitable service policies; equitable access; and accurate, unbiased, and courteous responses to all requests.

II. We uphold the principles of intellectual freedom and resist all efforts to censor library resources.

III. We protect each library user's right to privacy and confidentiality with respect to information sought or received and resources consulted, borrowed, acquired or transmitted.

IV. We recognize and respect intellectual property rights.

V. We treat co-workers and other colleagues with respect, fairness and good faith, and advocate conditions of employment that safeguard the rights and welfare of all employees of our institutions.

VI. We do not advance private interests at the expense of library users, colleagues, or our employing institutions.

VII. We distinguish between our personal convictions and professional duties and do not allow our personal beliefs to interfere with fair representation of the aims of our institutions or the provision of access to their information resources.

VIII. We strive for excellence in the profession by maintaining and enhancing our own knowledge and skills, by encouraging the professional development of co-workers, and by fostering the aspirations of potential members of the profession.

Adopted by the ALA Council

June 28, 1995

Reprinted with the permission of St. Mary's University Louis J. Blume Library

Bibliography

Ashworth, Wilfred (1979), *Special Libraries*, Clive Bingley, London.

Bloomfield, B. C. (1987), "Collection Development the Key Issues" in S. Conall, (Ed.), *Collection Development Options For efficient Management*, Tayler Graham, London.

British Standards Institution (1964), *Recommendations for the Preparation of Indexes For Books Periodicals and Other Publications*, London, (B. S. 3700: 1964).

Cutter, Charles Ami (1904), *Rules of a Dictionary Catalogue*, 4th ed., GPO, Washington.

Dougherty, R. M. and Hughes, (1991), *Preferred Futures for Libraries*, Research Libraries Group. Mountain View, California.

Esdaile A. (1969), *Esdaile's, Manual of Bibliography*, Allen and Unwin, London.

Evans, G. Edward (1987), *Developing Library and Information Centre Collections*, Libraries Unlimited, Littleton, Colorado.

Evans, G. Edward (2004), *Developing Library and Information Centre Collections*, 4th ed., Libraries Unlimited, Greenwood Pub., Colorado.

Geer, Helen Thoranton (1955), *Charging Systems*, ALA, Chicago.

Gelfand, M. A. (1974), *University Libraries for Developing Countries*, The University Book and Stationery, Delhi.

Hicks, Warren B and Alma, M Tillin (1970), *Developing Multimedia Libraries*, RR Bowker, New York.

Hutchins, Margaret (1944), *Introduction to Reference Work*, American Library Association, Chicago.

James, H.F. (1996), *Across the Generations: Selecting and Using Intergenerational Resources*, Highsmith Press, Fort Atkinson, WI.

Jugal Kishore (1981), *Personal Management in Libraries*, Ess Ess, Pub., New Delhi.

Katz, William A. (1980), Collection Development: The Selection of Materials for Libraries, Holt ,New York.

Khan, M. T. M. (1997), *Information Organization and Communication*, Ess Ess Publication, New Delhi..

Kingma, B.R., Irving, S. (1996), *The Economics of Access versus Ownership: The Costs and Benefits of Access to Scholarly Articles via Interlibrary Loan and Journal Subscription*, Haworth, New York, NY.

Kovacs, D. (2000), *Building Electronic Library Collections: The Essential Guide to Selection Criteria and Core Subject Collections*,, Neal-Schuman, New York, NY.

Krishna Kumar (1996), *Reference Service*, 5th rev. ed., Vikas Publication, New Delhi.

Lancaster, F. W., Collection Development in the year 2025.

Loertscher, D.V. (1996), *Collection Mapping in the LMC: Building Access in a World of Technology*, Hi Willow Research and Publishing, Castle Rock, CO.

Margrill and Garbin (1989), Acquisitions Management and Collection Development in Libraries, 2nd ed., ALA.

Margrill, Rose Mary and Hickery Doryalyn (1984), Acquisition Management and Collection Development, ALA, Chicago.

Mookerji, Radha Kumud (1969), *Ancient Indian Education*, 4th ed., Motilal Banarsidas, Delhi.

Narendra Nath (1973), *Promotion of Learning in India during Momammdan Rule*, Idarah-i-Adabiyat-i-Delhi, Delhi (Reprint).

Nazir Ahmad (1984), *Academic Libraries in Developing Society*, Qadiria, Lahore.

Pal, S. S. (2004), *Special Library System and Information Services*, Icon Pub., New Delhi.

Prasher, R. G. (2003), *Information and its Communication*, Medallion, Ludhiana.

Prasher, R.G (1991), *Managing University Libraries*, Today and Tomorrow's Pub., New Delhi.

Prasher, R.G. (1993), *Developing Library Collections*, Medellian, New Delhi.

Ranganathan, S. R. (1961), *Reference Service*, 2nd ed., Asia Publication, Bombay.

Ranganathan, S.R. (1988), *Library Manual*, 2nd ed., Sarada Ranganathan Endowment, Banglore.

Sankalia, H. D., (1972), *The University of Nalanda*, 2nd Rev. ed., Oriental Pub., Delhi.

Schammel, Aliran, Ed. (2001), *Handbook of Information Management*, Aslib-umi, London.

Sewa Singh (1986), *Reference Services In Academic Libraries in India*, Ess Ess Pub, New Delhi.

Sewa Singh, (1994), "Growth Development of University Libraries in India in : New Horizon in Library and Information Source, T & Publications, Madras.

Sharma, Jagdish Saran and Grover, D. R., (2004), *Reference Service and Sources of Information*, Ess Ess Publication, New Delhi.

Shera, Jessee H (1966), *Libraries and Organization of Knowledge*, Crosby, London.

Singh, S.P. and Krishna Kumar (2005), *Special Libraries in the Electronic Environment*, Bookwell, New Delhi.

Srivastava, Shyam Nath and Verma, Subash Chandra (1980), *University Libraries in India: Their Organization and Administration*, Sterling, New Delhi.

The ALA Glossary of Library and Information Science (1983), ALA, Chicago.

Thomsen, E. (1996), *Reference and Collection Development on the Internet: A How-To-Do-It Manual*, Neal-Schuman, New York, NY.

Trevens, W. Stanley (1887), *The Principles of Science*, Macmillan, London.

Vichery, B. C. (1965), *On Retrieval System Theory*, Buterworths, London.

Vishwanathan, C. G. (1972), *University Library of India : Principle and Policy*, New Delhi.

Voigt, M J. (1961), *Scientists Approaches to Information*, ALA, New York.

Wilson, L.R and Tauber, M.F. (1956), *The University Library*, Coloumbia Press, New York.

Wood, R.J., Hoffmann, F. (1996), *Library Development Policies: A Reference and Writers' Handbook*, Scarecrow, Lanham, MD.

Index